DESIGNED
TO **SUCCEED**
PROGRAMMED
TO **FAIL**

PRIYA CHIDANANDAN

 FriesenPress

Suite 300 - 990 Fort St
Victoria, BC, V8V 3K2
Canada

www.friesenpress.com

ISBN
978-1-5255-6448-2 (Hardcover)
978-1-5255-6449-9 (Paperback)
978-1-5255-6450-5 (eBook)

1. SELF-HELP

Distributed to the trade by The Ingram Book Company

TABLE OF CONTENTS

ACKNOWLEDGEMENT

My heartfelt gratitude to the great teachers from India, like Swami Vivekananda, Swami Rama and many others, who helped me understand the true essence of who we are, is at the core of our being. These teachers taught me, God is the goodness that exists within each one of us, and the divine exists in everything around us. I want to thank Ester Hicks, Jerry Hicks, and Abraham, for teaching me "The Law of Attraction" through their workshops and books. The teachings of Abraham helped me live a better life. My thanks to Oprah Winfrey for using television to impact and improve lives. Her words gave me the strength and courage to write this book. A big thank you to all my teachers, friends and family who encouraged me to write. Special thanks to my husband and son. The help I received for the final review and edit of this book from my son Rishab Nambiar, my friend Smita Prabhu and my niece Arya Pathak is greatly appreciated – thank you. This book is dedicated to my son Rishab Nambiar, whom I consider as God's greatest gift to me.

"Merrily, merrily, merrily, merrily, life is but a dream." Most of us grew up singing this beautiful song, but little do we realize the meaning of this line, until we have crossed a certain age. Each one of us has our own life experiences, which we handle differently. Our experiences give us a chance to learn and grow—to be better, or bitter, human beings—based on the choices we make. Some of us choose to view life as a glass half full, an outlook that gives us an opportunity to be better. Others choose to look at life as a glass half empty, and that creates the opportunity to become bitter. Some of us believe it is better to accept our fate, while others choose to shape their fate. Some of us choose to simply live, while others choose to thrive. It is these different choices we make that shapes our lives.

Looking back at my life, I asked myself why each one of us turns out differently, even though we go through similar circumstances. Some people do well, no matter how bad their environment, and they seem to thrive and succeed. What made these people succeed against all odds, while others stayed back?

Growing up, I was surrounded by some brilliant girls. They were the shining stars of their school. They demonstrated excellence in everything they undertook and had everything they needed to succeed in life. However, twenty years later, when I had turned to look back at life, these shining stars which I once looked up at, had stopped shining. What made the bright ones stop shining and the unexpected ones rise to succeed? After asking this question for several years, I finally have the answer.

How many of us have the courage to dream and fight to make our dreams come true? Though most of us dream, not many have the courage to fight the battles to make our dreams a reality. Most people allow their actions and decisions to be influenced by others around them, letting go of their dreams somewhere along the road.

At the root of all our lives are thoughts, beliefs, and rules. These rules and patterns of thinking are based in our societies, religions, and cultures, and they influence and impact lives across many generations, continuing to impact every human being today. Few people show the courage to move forward in life by breaking these boundaries. The majority, who believe what they are taught to believe, often stay back in life, doubting themselves and fail to succeed. Often our vision does not take us far beyond the practices and beliefs we grew up with. When this happens, we give in and follow what we are told to follow, because we believe those around us more than we believe in ourselves.

To make the leap in life and break the old pattern of thoughts and behaviors, we need to have the courage to push ourselves and those around us, who are doubting the vision we have for our lives. We hold ourselves back at various turning points in our lives because we doubt ourselves, or fear others around us. We are all too comfortable listening and following instructions because we have practiced it all our lives. What we have not been taught, to practice is courage. Kids who grow up to bring a change in this world are either brought up by parents who encourage them to question and explore everything they come across in life, or they are kids who, by nature, explore without fear—no matter what the consequences. The rest of us follow the trail and live lives that are not too different from how we are taught to live, by those who raised us. Each generation teaches the next generation the same old ways, keeping us all in an infinite cycle of beliefs and practices that do not serve us.

I recall an incident that took place in my life, when I was around three years old. While playing inside the house one morning, I picked up something from the cupboard to look at. The next minute,

I dropped it, and it broke. I cannot recall what it was, but what followed has stayed in my memory ever since. My father saw it happen and asked me to apologize. He asked me to say, "I will never do it again." I did not intend to break it, and I could not promise him such an accident will never occur again, and so I refused. He asked me repeatedly, and as time went by, his anger and my stubbornness grew stronger. Eventually, he stepped outside to break off a branch of a tree from the backyard to hit me with. This type of tree is supposed to have the most flexible wood, making it hard to break, but he broke off a cane and started hitting me with it. As he hit me, he asked me to apologize, but by now, I was too stubborn. I was not willing to apologize, no matter what happened. The cane, which was not supposed to break, broke into pieces in the process, and my father left me to go out and get a second piece of cane. Fearing what might happen to me, my mother and aunt picked me up and hid me from him, before he returned. My leg was bruised from top down, with red marks from the cane, but I had no regrets or fear. I do not recall my father hitting me like that ever again.

Today, when I look back at that incident, in addition to my extreme stubbornness, what I see in my three-year-old self is extreme courage. Though my stubbornness was not too helpful in my childhood, my courage has been the biggest strength of my life. It helped me break boundaries and take the leap, even when the whole world was against me.

We do not consider how much courage plays a role in our lives, and the importance of cultivating courage in our children. Each one of us needs to be the best version of ourselves and teach our children to be the best version of themselves. We need to watch our children and guide them and give them room to grow in their own way. Look around you and watch the different kinds of trees that grow. Just like a plum tree is different from an avocado tree, each child is different and unique. If we have a plum tree, and we fail to understand it is a plum tree and fertilize it with the wrong fertilizer, the plum tree will not thrive. Unfortunately, we often deal with our children in this manner. We guide our children without quite understanding them, and we make decisions based on our assumptions about them. Instead, we need to understand our children before we give them guidance in life. Let us give them a chance to be themselves and watch the miracle unfold. It requires real courage to step back and let go of control like this, correcting and guiding them based on who they truly are. When we fail to cultivate courage in our kids, when we value cultural and social practices more than our kids, and when we ask our kids to take the path, we want them to take, our kids stop shining—we blow out their light. If we fail to give them room to shine and be themselves, they will only exist and never thrive enough to experience the sweetness of life. This is what happened to many girls I have come across in life. Their light was blown out since no one gave their dreams a chance. Social, cultural, and religious factors worked against most of these girls I came across, and they lived the lives their parents wanted them to live. Now, more than twenty years later, they live with their dreams sunk down in their hearts, and regret and unhappiness in their eyes.

Human beings fear the unknown and are comfortable with the familiar. Even if the familiar is not what we want and exploring the unknown might accomplish our dream, we tend to stick with what we know rather than face our fear of the unknown.

When old practices do not make sense, we fail to choose new ways, since we worry about how others around us will perceive us if we break out of it. When people begin to measure self-worth through the eyes of others, it becomes a breeding ground for ego. We attach ourselves with things around us, which creates the need to satisfy our ego through ownership and control. This is a typical characteristic of an egocentric mind. The egocentric mind causes us to look at ourselves and the world differently. It gives us a different perspective and takes us down the wrong track in life. If seeking lasting happiness and joy in life, we need to abandon our old ways of thinking. We need to listen to our hearts and not to our ego. We must follow some more positive rules to be joyful in life. Like a muscle in a human body, happiness can be developed with practice. By abandoning our old ways, and adopting new and positive ways of thinking, we can transform our lives, and fill it with joy.

CHAPTER 1

THINK BEFORE YOU ACT

I was born in a beautiful village in the South Indian state of Kerala. Kerala closely resembles Hawaii in vegetation, climate, and natural beauty. In this part of the Indian sub-continent, people are well educated and information hungry. They can do without their morning coffee, but they cannot do without reading the morning newspaper. It is a place unique in many ways, including its natural beauty.

My mother was the eldest girl of her family, and I was the first child to mark the next generation of mine. We lived in a joint-family system at that time, and I was surrounded by many of my maternal family members. My family belonged to the Nair community, which is one of the few matriarchal societies that still exists. I grew up like a tomboy, pampered and spoiled, with lots of love from everyone in the community—family and neighbors. I feared nothing, and I was very curious. I loved challenges and exploring new places and things in our beautiful village with the other kids in my neighborhood.

My favorite people in my family were my grandfather and great grandmother. They were the most loving souls I had ever come across in my life. I was very attached to these two, as I follow them around as their little assistant.

My great grandmother had a morning routine. She used to wake up early, take a shower, and pray to the rising sun before she began her day. If I woke up early enough, I used to pray with her, mimicking her actions and watching her throughout her prayers.

She used to chant mantras watching the rising sun, and sometimes I used to see tears of joy slid down her cheeks. At dusk, she used to meditate, and I used to sit with her. It was like I could see her body, but she was somewhere else - like her awareness had left her body. I recall staring at her and wondering where she had gone, even though I could see her still body next to me. At night, after dinner, she used to tell me stories from the Indian scripture, Bhagavatam. She would speak of Gods and Goddesses coming to Earth to destroy evil and sustain truth and justice. She also told me stories from the Indian epics, like Ramayana and Mahabharata. The choice was mine, every night, as to what I wanted to hear. I enjoyed listening to these stories as I fell asleep.

My other favorite person in the family– my grandfather, was retired and enjoyed farming. I accompanied him in all his work, which included taking food for the farmers working in the fields, and keeping an eye on the crops, from sowing to replanting. We made sure that the seeds, once sown, were safe until they germinated, and the seedlings grew healthy and were ready to replant. My grandfather and I also prepared a vegetable patch in our backyard every summer. He used to teach me how to sow the seeds, protect them from birds and bugs, add organic fertilizers, provide support for the plants, and harvest them when ready. We used to water the vegetables, check on the health of the plants, look for any bugs and diseases, and if present, bring issues under control in an organic way. *"The first vegetable that shows up on the plant is usually the healthiest, so do not pluck it. We will collect its seeds for next year."* I still remember my grandfather's words. By age five, I knew so much about organic gardening and growing plants and vegetables, that I continue to use all that knowledge today in my backyard kitchen garden. Every time I get into a problem with gardening, some forgotten memory comes back, and I always have the solution.

After his days' work, my grandfather used to rest in his easy chair (like a hammock, made with a wooden stand and cloth). He relaxed in this chair and took a nap every day after lunch. My grandfather would snore very loudly during sleep, which was very amusing to me. I used to crawl under the chair and listen to him snore when he napped. His snore had a certain rhythm to it, which I found interesting, and more than anything else, I used to wonder how someone could possibly make all that noise when they were fast asleep.

One day, while under my grandfather's easy chair, listening to his amusing snore, my eyes fell on the way the chair was built. I was curious how a piece of cloth and some wood was holding the weight of my heavy grandfather. After my grandfather woke up, I asked him how the chair worked and what each of the wooden structures did. I never got a good answer, even after asking him multiple times, so I decided I would find out for myself. The next day, when my grandfather was sleeping, I crawled under the chair determined to find out. As I tried to move various wooden pieces to see what each part did, my eyes fell on two long, circular sticks. *That wood looks interesting. What does it do?* I thought. I needed to find out, and so I pulled on them. The easy chair collapsed, and I quickly jumped out from under it, but my poor grandfather fell in. I do not recall what happened next, except my grandfather's loud cry for help. In the middle of his deep sleep, he was totally unaware of what was happening to him. I fled the place like an arrow shot from a bow, fearing the consequences, and feeling guilty. I felt terrible about what happened to my grandfather, but luckily, he was fine. A few hours later, when I returned home full of guilt, my grandfather said, in a loud and loving voice, "*You knocked me down. Don't do it again.*"

Many such incidents happened in my childhood, where I learned things the hard way when I failed to get an answer. I could not stop being curious. I was never satisfied with basic answers like, "That's the way it is." I had to know why, and I needed to be able to reason and understand it for myself. My curiosity, coupled with my courage, helped me to fight some of the biggest battles in my life. It helped me take the leap to this life I am living today. My curiosity made me question and try to reason everything. I never bought into anything just because somebody who was close to me said so. To me, it did not matter who said it; I needed to find out why things were the way they were and if it really made sense. If I understood and felt it to be right, I accepted it. If not, I refused to accept it or follow along. I paid attention to my inner voice and to those who I felt spoke the truth. The rest I questioned, reasoned, and if I wasn't convinced, I showed the courage to walk away.

When I was seven years old, my family moved out of our ancestral house to a new house in the city, owned by my parents. I missed everything - my old home, the beautiful village, my friends, and more than anything else, the loving people I had around me. Growing up in that large family, I never got a chance to get to know my parents well because the rest of the family attended to all my needs. Now, in my new home, my parents and my three-year-old brother were the only people around me. My mother was having a hard time managing her full-time job as a teacher in addition to managing a home and two kids. In the joint-family system, she had lots of help. Here she had none, my father never cared much about her difficulties or our upbringing.

Together, my parents treated my brother as special. They bought and did things for him and not for me. As any kid would, I was angry and sad when my parents acted this way. When I complained, they said they were doing it because he was the baby of the family, and so he was special. I was hardly four years older than my brother, but I believed this reasoning for a while. After three or four years, I noticed they were still doing this. I asked again, and I was told he would always get special treatment, no matter his age, because he was younger—they spoke as if that was justification. But when I started questioning their actions, the truth came to light. They said, *"He is a boy, and boys are special."*

My father saw me as a responsibility that he needed to get married-off once I came of age. His outlook was that girls were not of much value to a family and not good enough. My parents never believed that I was capable because I was a girl. Instead, they had high hopes for my brother. I was sad, angry, and confused at the same time, and found it hard to accept their views about me and girls.

At our old house, no one told me I was different or lesser than any of the boys around. In fact, there were lots of boys in our neighborhood who were older than me yet far less capable in many ways. *My parents cannot be right*, I thought.

I started observing the boys and girls around me. I noticed that, irrespective of gender, some seemed to be better than others in different areas. Gender did not determine academic performance or other skill sets, in my observation. What my parents were telling me just did not make sense to me. So, I disagreed, and when they tried to impose this belief on me, I rebelled.

As I grew older, I saw this belief as a genuine lack of understanding on my parents' part. I tried to convince my parents that, in the modern world, a girl and a boy can be equally successful if given an opportunity for education. But they did not want to listen. They were so strongly rooted in their belief, and their ears and minds were closed to my explanations. Realizing that I could not change their beliefs, I stopped trying to convince them. Slowly, I learned to ignore and walk away, even though some of their remarks hurt me deeply.

I started paying attention to other families and girls around me. I came across a few cases of gender discrimination that were far worse than mine, and to my surprise, those girls were not complaining. It was shocking to see that these girls were silently taking it. At first, I could not understand why this was happening. *Why would someone put up with such treatment, without so much as a word?* Soon, I realized that they were not thinking the way I was. They failed to question and reason, and they lacked a level of courage and curiosity. They simply believed what they were told. "Parents cannot be wrong, and everything they do is for our good." This is what many of us were taught while growing up. Many girls believed this teaching, and in my experience, many of those who didn't believe this teaching, lacked the courage to speak up.

As I grew up, I noticed that, while some countries were impacted more than others, this was a global problem. Initially, I thought it had something to do with time, place, education, and other factors. However, I found that there is only one thing causing the issue of gender discrimination and inequality— failure to think and reason for ourselves, instead believing what we are told, and following in the steps of past generations.

When people lack the ability to question and reason what they hear, they become followers. Our silence in the face of such discrimination only contributes to the problem. Silence is an implicit approval. Since most of the girls around me were silent to the discrimination, the belief of the people and the society—that females are weak and that their treatment of girls and women is "right" and fair—grew stronger.

In parts of the world where strong patriarchal societies flourish, when a woman becomes pregnant, the family will wish for a boy. When my mother was pregnant with me, few people in the society had the same wish. They told my mother she would be blessed with a boy. The words and wishes of these people instilled in my parents, the feeling that having a girl child was a bad thing. And when I was born, though my mother loved me, that feeling in her persisted. Three years later, when my brother was born, my parents felt he was the child to be proud of. The difference in gender meant a world of difference to them, and the difference they felt was visible in their treatment of us, growing up.

This belief that boys are superior, and behavior of the parents towards their girls treating her as less worthy, is driven by our capacity to think and reason more than anything else. A good example in my own family, who proved this to me was my maternal grandmother, who educated all her daughters the same as her sons. During a time when girls were not sent to college and were married off as teenagers, my grandmother, with the support of my grandfather, educating her daughters, and gave them the choice and the opportunity for a career. However, my parents who were more educated than my grandparents, allowed themselves to be influenced by people with gender-biased attitude.

Thinking and reasoning play key roles in our everyday lives. When we fail to think, we fail to teach our kids the importance of thinking and reasoning. Instead, we teach our kids to follow, perpetuating the cycle of outdated social practices, creating an infinite loop, generation after generation. When girls are treated as second-class human beings, boys in such families and communities grow up to be disrespectful toward women and girls. These boys grow up and pass on the same beliefs to their sons, and the cycle continues.

The truth about any situation can only be seen if we are willing to use our own minds instead of following others. We need to view everything with an open mind, without letting ego, pride, or fear get in our way. Unless we focus on teaching our children to think for themselves, these issues will persist, and the cycle will continue.

We have been taught by our society that we are born knowing nothing, and we need to learn everything from people around us. What we see and hear from the adults in our lives is the ultimate truth, and we must learn everything from parents, teachers, and others who have lived longer than us and know better than we do. Our ego reacts strongly when our kids question us, even if it is out of curiosity. In most cases, when we are questioned, instead of encouraging kids to think outside the box, we react negatively, because our ego dislikes being questioned. This is a fool-proof method for creating outdated cyclical and generational patterns of thoughts and actions. Whenever I questioned my parents' gender bias, I got the same pattern of response from them. Human beings are addicted to being right, and it is hard for most parents to see that they are wrong, especially when it is their own child questioning or opposing them. In my case, if my parents had displayed the willingness to listen to me, they would have seen for themselves that their beliefs were wrong. It was their belief that my brother, being a boy, would be their strength and support, whereas I, being a girl, was weak and ignorant. Because of this, they treated him one way and me another. This is conditional love caused by ego and blind belief.

Just because we brought our kids into the world, does not mean our thoughts and beliefs about our children is always right. Parents do not always know better than their kids. If that were true, our kids would never outsmart us. However, our kids often outsmart us in many ways in life, because awareness and experience are two different entities. Though experience is helpful, without awareness, we fail to see the truth. The lack of awareness in us makes us reject the truth in our lives. A parent who is aware will never discriminate against their children based on their gender. A country that is aware will not discriminate against its citizens based on race or religion. The absence of awareness and strong ego is what makes humans discriminate against each other.

The ego is like negative energy; it wipes truth, love, and compassion out of our system. It gives us a boost when we think of ourselves as the best and others as less than us. Ego constantly compare us with others, which gives us either a sense of false pride, or a sense of shame and causes us to focus on how others might perceive us.

The ego goes above and beyond to protect the feeling of pride, and because it causes us to become overly concerned about how others perceive us, we then do everything in our power to keep our social image at its best. In many countries, ego makes fathers feel inferior when a female child is born into their family. Where ego exists, love diminishes—or vanishes—and we hurt others. Ego generates our self-beliefs, which can override our awareness of our actions. Ego makes us hungry for power and superiority, which can lead us to inflict pain on others, all in justification of our actions.

.

Though religions and cultures around the world are all based on great principles, with the intention of improving the lives of human beings, today the outcomes seem to be contrary to the initial intentions. Religious teachings have been mistranslated and misinterpreted with selfish motives to control humanity. Today, these teachings and practices have become strong pillars of egocentric beliefs and practices. If we think with an open mind, we can find out the truth behind these teachings, but no one seems to be interested in the truth. Humanity is caught up in the never-ending cycle of listening, following, believing, and controlling, all generated by ego.

How do we stop our ego? It is simple. Every time a thought comes to you, reflect on that thought and ask yourself if it is generated from the loving part of you or from a place of fear or control. Reflecting on the origin of a thought will give you a clearer picture of what is going on within you, relative to the thoughts you experience.

Thought and reason are behind all inventions—big and small. Thoughts can create peace movements, just as they can create war. Thoughts keep us informed and curious, and they govern everything in our lives. They impact how we live and what we achieve in our lives. Both the good and the bad that we witness all around us are a result of our thoughts. How we think makes us what we are, yet there is a big percentage of us who prefer to believe what we are told, without a good thought. We train our kids, from a very young age, to follow *our* path, not understanding the importance of teaching them to think for themselves and discover their own path and purpose in life.

The root cause of all major issues is lack of ability to think. It is time we ask some basic questions about our way of life, rather than just believing what we are told and following others. Why do we expect everything that worked in the past to work now? Times have changed. We need to stop believing that everything that has been practiced so far is the best working model. Let me ask you something: When you get a new model of a gadget (be it a phone, watch, or anything else), do you throw the new model away and continue to use the old model? Just because your parents and grandparents wore the old model of watch or drove the old model of car, will you refuse to try the new model? I am sure you will choose the new model. Why, then, are we sticking to old models when it comes to our thoughts and behaviors? We should adapt our actions and think based on the time and circumstances in which we live. Ask yourself if the old ways make sense. If they don't, search for what does. If the old ways are outdated, find new ways. It's time we all think before we act. *Think* is a magic word. Thoughts can transform people, families, societies, and the entire planet. It is time we give this wonderful five-letter word the place it deserves in our lives.

CHAPTER 2

THE QUALITY OF OUR THOUGHTS GOVERN THE QUALITY OF OUR LIVES

Thoughts create the world, and our thoughts decide our destiny. Our success in life, and our happiness, has a lot to do with the way we choose to think. Successful people think differently when compared to the rest. People who think positively and live with love and gratitude, experience the world differently than those who view life negatively. When we view life negatively our thoughts are negative, and it results in an unhappy life. On the other hand, a positive outlook in life rewards you with a happy, healthy life.

Looking out at my garden the other day, I realized that every seed I planted, and the look of my garden, was all just a thought, once upon a time. My garden is nothing but the manifestation of my thoughts into reality, which I accomplished through my actions. My thought was the seed of the creation that is now the physical reality that is my garden. If you look around, you will notice that most of what exists around you, are manifestations of thoughts. The homes we live in, the clothes we wear, the cars we drive—everything exists because someone thought of it first and later brought it to fruition through action.

Thoughts not only play a key role in our day to day life, but also have a direct impact on our physical wellbeing. We live in an era where people are more focused on good health, than ever before. We care about what we eat and drink, and we take care of our physical health. Healthy living has become a key focus in modern times. However, we are missing out on one major factor when it comes to healthy living: our thoughts. What have thoughts got to do with health?

Studies show that negative thoughts can cause many physical issues and diseases in our body. Doctor and scientist Dr. Joe Dispenza write about how negative thoughts can create diseases in his book "Becoming Supernatural". He explains stress in a whole new way in the following words. *"The moment we react to any conditions in the outer world that tends to be threatening, whether the threat is real or imagined, our body releases stress hormones in order to mobilize enormous amounts of energy in response to that threat. When this occurs, the body moves out of balance – that's exactly what stress is."*[1] He goes on to explain how stress impacts us, *"When we are living in survival mode and these hormones of stress like adrenaline and cortisol keep pumping through our body, we stay on high alert instead of returning to balance."* *"When this imbalance is maintained long term chances are, we are headed for disease, because long term stress down regulates healthy expression of genes."*[2] Through his research, he has observed how negative thoughts can cause diseases and how positive thoughts can improve our health and wellbeing.

Various other studies have led many scientists to similar conclusions about the importance of thoughts and their effects on the human body. We can alter our internal system to generate a stress response through thinking stressful thoughts. In other words, we can trigger our stress response with our thoughts alone—even in the most beautiful of moments. For example, imagine you are taking a perfect vacation in Hawaii, on a nice sunny day. The weather is perfect, and you are lying on the beach with the crystal-clear water touching your feet. Five minutes after settling into this memorable moment, your mind travels back in time, to an incident that happened at work last week. Now, sitting in this perfect, beautiful place you are thinking about that issue, which is triggering your internal stress response.

There is nothing wrong in thinking about a solution to a problem during moments of relaxation. After all, when we are in a positive state of mind, we often come up with the best solutions. However, our intention should be to resolve the situation and return to the present moment. Unfortunately, this is not what most people do. We often get stuck in the situation we are ruminating on, and that ruins our present state of being, sometimes during the most wonderful moments of our lives.

Most people—no matter how much joy and beauty exists around—do not invest their attention in the present moment. Instead, we tend to put our attention elsewhere—in the past or future. We replay negative situations repeatedly in our memory, thus continually robbing ourselves of present happiness and placing ourselves in a state of stress.

We live in a society fueled by money, power, and competition, and we are constantly in a rat race to get to the top. Animals, on the other hand, can live in the "now"—the present moment. For e.g. In the rainforest many of the big cats like lion and tiger compete for food, chasing and hunting down smaller animals. When hungry, they compete for food with their own kind, if there is shortage of food, and once their need for food is met, they are back in a present, blissful state. But humans have a more highly developed brain compared to other species. We think, plan, and create, all of which are great skills if used correctly, but are we using our abilities the right way?

Most of us have lost control of the thinking mechanism within us. We live in the clutches of a thought-centric world that constantly puts our minds in the past or the future, keeping us in stressful states and never in the present. This creates stress, anxiety, fear, anger, and all the problems we are seeing in the world today—all fueled by something as simple as our thoughts, which have taken over our lives. We fear people who are different from us; we imagine things that are not necessarily true, based on partial facts or blind beliefs. And the list goes on. Our perception is based on our thought or imagination of situations. For example, when a person responds poorly to something, due to an issue in their personal life, we misinterpret that and create a whole narrative behind their response. We live thinking that we know everything about the other person, and judge everything and everyone based on our assumed understanding. By doing this, we complicate our thought process and invite stress into our lives.

Taking a detour from our unhealthy thought patterns and putting our thoughts and internal mechanism to work in the right way, is crucial for our overall well-being. Awareness is the only tool we need to make this happen. We need to be aware of our thoughts and disconnect from negative thoughts.

Every time we catch ourselves thinking negative thoughts, we must identify if the thought is good or bad for us, using our emotions. Emotions are our guide to internal well-being. Why? Because "good" thoughts and emotions put the body's internal mechanism in a state of balance and coherent energy which makes you both healthy and happy.

If our thoughts are not making us feel good, and we are aware that they are being caused by negative emotions, be aware that the thought could trigger our stress response. When this awareness comes to us, make it a practice of switching out of negative thoughts. If we can practice this simple exercise of switching a negative thought into a positive one, this will bring a profound change to our health and happiness. Switching out of negative thought is not very difficult, you just need to find out which positive thoughts work best for you to practice this exercise. In my case I focus on nature since I love nature. The minute I catch my mind crossing over to territories of negative thoughts and emotions, I take a walk out in nature or look outside the window and find something that fills me with joy and wonder. It can be a bird that is chirping on a tree, the cloud formation in the sky, the beauty of a tree outside or anything in nature. If we find a good thought or object to focus on and come out of negative thoughts and emotions, over time, we will develop a habit of positive thinking and negative thoughts will bother us less in our life. Slowly but surely, we will think more positive thoughts, which will create positive emotions and good health, and we will have a healthy and happy life.

If a negative thought is sticking to us, and we are unable to stop the thought, we can shift our attention to our breath. With a singular focus on our breath, we draw attention away from the negative thought. Practice doing this until you feel calm and the thought is disconnected.

Each person is a bundle of loving energy. Our hearts, lungs, and every organ in our bodies is energized and functioning, from the time we were in our mother's womb, to this very moment. Breath is like a rope that ties life to the body. Feel the breath and be aware of it, realizing that we have been breathing with such ease, non-stop, for years. Know the importance of breath and how it holds life in our bodies and focus on it, to get out of negative thoughts.

Getting out of painful, negative situations is often easier said than done. People talk about "facing the pain" to get out of it, but in my experience, remembering only intensifies the pain. What worked for me was accepting my circumstance and life with an understanding that we are all truly divine. Out of my pain, I found a way of accepting what had happened, without focusing on the details of the experience. In my case, the lack of love I experienced, is something I learned to accept. I also learned to accept the way my parents are, and that it is wrong of me to expect them to change. I understood that their life is governed by their beliefs, and lack of understanding made them think and act in ways that hurt me. I know who I am, I know that I am a good person, and that is good enough for me. It is my parents' choice how they want to perceive me. Whatever they believe about me is no more than their beliefs — it does not make it true. They have the right to choose, and so do I. I choose to care about the life that has been gifted to me. I choose to stand up for myself and remind myself who I am. I am not defined by the narrative of others, including that of my parents.

My journey from negative emotions and pain to positivity and wellness came from a memory of my great grandmother. As a child, I was around her all the time. I noticed she would constantly chant a word: "Narayana", the name of a Hindu God. She would do this almost all day when she was not engaged in a task or conversation. It wasn't that she was always happy—she had her moments of sadness—but what I took notice of, was that, if any moment of sadness or worry overcame her, she would start chanting this word, and she would slowly bounce back to a positive state. Years later, when I was consumed with emotional pain, I started to chant—just like her—every time I experienced fear, anger, or other negative emotions. Slowly, this simple practice worked wonders in me, keeping me free of painful thoughts. After years of struggling with my emotions, I have found peace within, through this simple exercise. When I catch myself thinking about certain past incidents, I either chant the very same word that I heard my great grandmother chant, or I focus on my breath and life energy, both of which cut off that negative thought.

I often reflect on my life before I started this practice, and I see my previous self as an emotional addict. I could not forgive or forget some of the people in my life for what they had done to me. Family members acted selfishly and not only put my life in jeopardy, but turned around and accused me of many things, which I never did or said. I could not come to terms with this behavior, and I felt extremely betrayed. I started to recall the memories every day, and I worked myself into a state of emotional addiction. This manifested in many symptoms, including constant chill, fatigue, heart palpitations, vertigo, and more. I made frequent visits to my doctor, who ran all kinds of tests on me, all of which had negative results. Finally, my doctor asked me, *"Priya, are you stressed?"* I wasn't sure how to answer. I hadn't considered that my emotional state was the root cause of my physical symptoms.

If our thoughts and negative emotions are out of control, our bodies receive an overdose of stress hormones. These hormones impact our internal organs, which impacts our health in the long run, causing various diseases. This is exactly where I was heading, at that point in my life.

When we see how our internal stress response gets triggered by our thoughts, we become clear about the importance of happiness in our daily lives. Most of the world is unhappy, and we need to be happy to be healthy. If we can be aware of our thoughts and make it a habit of thinking positive thoughts, we will experience positive emotions, which will generate well-being in and around us. When we feel good physically, mentally, and emotionally, and we respond to the world around us positively, we get positive responses most of the time. Our world becomes more positive, since that is the energy we are putting out into the world. Others will begin enjoying our company and see us as the positive people we are. Our interactions with the world will be better, and these positive interactions will allow us to deal with situations in our lives far better, than what we usually do. The change in us, will bring success and happiness into our lives much faster than otherwise. Our lives will slowly start to change, all because we chose to change one thing—our thoughts.

CHAPTER 3

LOVE, FREEDOM AND HAPPINESS

Homeless people wandering the streets, was a very common sight during my childhood, growing up in India. Some of these people lived as families in tents near the street, and among these "families" were kids. I used to watch these kids every morning on my way to school, and many of them looked happy, even though they had very little. They smiled and played near the tent next to their parents, who fed them with the little they had. I used to wonder, what made them happy when they had nothing in life? Now I know that these kids had everything they really needed to be happy. Their parents took care of them, fed them, loved them. It was the love of their parents and the freedom to be themselves, that gave them so much happiness. The shabby clothes they wore and the tents that were their homes did not really bother them. They were content inside, despite how poor they were, compared to the outside world around them. At that time, however, I did not realize this truth. I saw them as helpless kids, and I decided that, when I grew up, I wanted to help the poor.

One day, at the breakfast table, I told my parents that I want to help the poor when I grow up. My parents laughed at me. They said, *"You are supposed to get married and raise a family. Besides, girls are not smart enough for such things."* They gave such responses whenever I talked about my plans and dreams for the future. When I became a teenager, they started having conversations about my marriage. I told them I had no interest in marriage; I wanted to complete my education. My parents paid no attention to this and continued the discussion of my marriage. They conveyed the message, that I had no choice, in numerous ways - both directly and indirectly. It was like my life belonged to my parents. Since I was a girl, they could decide what to do with my life. They made me feel like only my brother had the right to wish or dream, since he was a boy, and what would become of my life was not my choice, all because I was a girl.

I hated the very thought of marriage without education and financial independence. I wanted to put my life to use in more ways than just taking care of a family. I could not imagine devoting my entire life to cooking, cleaning, and taking care of a family, and do nothing more. Instead, I felt a burning desire to be something or do something in this life. I had no idea what that something was; all I knew was that my life should be my choice. I wanted to complete education and become independent. However, my parents had different plans for me, which went against what I wanted. Seeing my passion and drive to succeed, my parents tried to convince me that I was not capable of succeeding. *"A woman cannot be independent, and her duty is to take care of a family"*, they tried hammering this belief into me. They used to tell me, it is a struggle to succeed and I was incapable of succeeding. "If that is the case, I love the struggle and I know I will succeed", I told them. I also asked my mother why she is not quitting her job if she truly believed what she is saying, to which she had no answer. Once my mother told me that a woman cannot live without the help of a man, but even while she said it, I knew she never believed it herself. I knew these were all statements she is making based on what my father wanted.

I knew the reason my parents were imposing this belief on me, was to get me married off as soon as possible and get done with the responsibility they had towards me. Many incidents that took place at home gave me the feeling that I was unwanted. One example was when my father put a picture of my brother on the fridge, and my brother asked why they only had his picture up there. My father's response was, *"Everything here belongs to you, and you are important. That's why."* I immediately thought, *What about me?* I was afraid to verbalize this, as I already knew the answer to my question—I was not important.

My earliest memory of such an incident was when I was three years old. In our culture, at three years old, every child has a writing ceremony, where the father helps the child write letters on a plate filled with rice. The child is seated on their father's lap and the father holds the child's hand and writes the first few letters of our language - Malayalam. This ceremony marks the beginning of the child's education, and it is held on an auspicious day, at a precise time, to symbolize that the child will be well educated. For my ceremony, my father was not even present; he went to work, as usual. He did not care about the ceremony or my education. A girl's education did not mean much to him. Since my father was not present, my grandfather took his place. He put me in his lap and made me write the letters. My maternal grandparents, aunts and uncles made this event a celebration at our home. A few years later, when it was my brother's turn, my father made it a big deal of this ceremony. He took our family to one of the most auspicious temples—that of the goddess of knowledge— miles away from our home. My father made sure my brother's writing ceremony was done in the best way possible, all because he was a boy.

Growing up and experiencing this gender bias, I thought my parents disliked me. But there were times when they seemed to care for me. For example, whenever I would come home late from school, my mother would always be worried. She would often stand on the front porch, looking and waiting for me. My mother did a lot for me—taking care of me and doing all her household chores, without any help. My father often instructed her to make me do the housework too, since he believed that the purpose of my life—a woman's life— was to take care of a family. Seeing my passion for studies, and being a teacher herself, my mother let me focus on my books and took care of the housework on her own. But I could clearly see her obsession with my brother, which left her with little love for me.

My father on the other hand occasionally showered me with insane amount of love, though I could hardly see any love in his actions towards me. This confused me since his words and actions never matched. Today when I look back, I know why he acted this way – it was a clever way of manipulating and controlling me.

Often my parents acted in ways that hurt me, and sometimes it was hard to take. Once, when I got hurt beyond what I could handle, I said, *"If you didn't want me, why did you bring me up? You should have put me in an orphanage or killed me before birth."* I said this out of intense pain, but my speaking out had my parents questioning whether they had disciplined me enough. They believed they had provided everything for me, and I was being so mean to them. I cannot imagine how rude my words sounded or how hurt they felt, but the words exploded from a place of intense emotional wound. A place of feeling unwanted by my own parents. Some girls are abused for saying such things to their parents, but in my case, the few times my father tried to hit me, I would stand still like a stone. My inner strength and courage could overcome anything, and my parents knew they could not do much. They saw me as a spoiled, arrogant girl whom they failed to discipline because I was too strong. Yes, I was strong. Every time I faced intense pain, injustice, or unfair behavior, strength and courage filled my system. It was like every cell in my body knew I was standing for the truth, and there was absolutely nothing to fear in that. However, if I had the slightest amount of guilt, this courage would not show up.

My parents thought that taking away the freedom of a girl—treating her as lesser being—was the right way to bring up girls. They believed girls had no right to equality and lacked intelligence and ability when compared to, boys who were superior. My reactions to their painful words and actions, my courage, and my dreams of being independent were all perceived negatively. Their response and reactions towards me, made me want to prove myself, because I thought my parents behaved this way out of a genuine lack of understanding. I thought I can correct their outlook towards girls and me, if I become independent and prove them wrong. I hoped and believed, that they would someday see their mistakes and turn around and love and accept me. However, I was wrong. Years later I learned one of the biggest lessons of my life - you can never change others when their minds are closed and filled with ego. An egoic mind will never allow a person to accept their mistakes. Instead, they will always try to prove themselves right, by justifying their mistakes, due to false pride. It took me a long time to understand this truth and stop expecting love and acceptance from them or anyone else. I realized the only person I can change is myself.

At school, my teachers encouraged me, and they saw talent and leadership qualities in me. At home, things were different. Often my parents would try to put me down when I participated in conversations or discussions at home. Everything my brother said or did was encouraged and seen as brilliant, whereas most of what I said or did was perceived as foolish, without a good thought. I felt insulted and belittled during such times, and I gradually avoided having conversations with my family. I lived in my room with my books. We all lived under the same roof, but mentally, I was miles away from them. Fear and anger used to fill me after most conversations with my family, and I used to go to my room and focus on my books or cry, since the pain and insult was too much to take at times. One day, after such a conversation, I was alone in my room crying when my eyes fell on a picture that hung on the wall. It was the picture of the Goddess Mahalakshmi, and I felt the image was smiling at me. I kept staring at it, since I felt something strange about what was going on. As the picture of the goddess continued smiling, I started having mental conversations with the image, and the pain in my heart poured out. I asked questions like, *why do my parents dislike me so much, because I am a girl?* and immediately receive a response in my mind. Most of the answers were along the lines of, *I am here for you. When God is with you, why do you need anyone else?* My teenage brain told me I was crazy to ask questions to a picture and answer the questions myself. But I felt great relief after every conversation with this image, so I never cared too much about what was going on. Every time I felt hurt and sat in my room feeling sad, this picture would smile, and a mental conversation would follow which made me feel better. Slowly, my parents' words and actions began to bother me less and I felt safe and loved by a divine loving energy which flowed to me through this image.

I spent hours in my room, by myself, with my books and the image of the goddess with whom I would have mental conversations. My curious mind went in various directions. Sometimes I was curious about God, sometimes about life, and sometimes about various events around me, that did not make sense. When I have a question in my mind and look at this image sometimes, I get a thought or memory that gave me a clue to the answer, other times all I got was just a smile. Life is a mystery, and I know I cannot receive all the answers. So, over time, I have learned to enjoy the mysterious nature of life.

My father would bring up family discussions with an intention of getting me to obey him. He would discuss how children who refuse to obey their parents would end up in bad places in life, because of their bad karma of hurting parents. He would point out many examples from family and society to prove his point. However, I could clearly see these examples had nothing to do with listening and obeying parents, though I never said a word against him. I also understood that the insane amount of love he is occasionally showering on me was a well thought out strategy. When someone loves us, we start trusting them. Trust gives access and control if they succeed in convincing us that their love is real. My father was trying to manipulate me using love and trust, to achieve what he wanted out of me. "Is he? Can parents do such things to their children?" I was not sure at that time.

Twelve years later I saw a mother who used the same technique to manipulate her son who loved her more than life itself. She like my father cared more about herself and less about her son. To achieve what she desired she engaged in a lot of wrong doings, without any consideration for her son and his family. After I witnessed this incident, I could see through my father's words and actions – his intentions were clear to me.

In many cultures' children are taught to trust and obey parents and to please them. A child who does this is labeled a good child. Though majority of the parents are extremely loving, there is at least a small percentage of parents who care more about themselves and less about their children. In such cases these teaching can be misleading. We need to teach children to be wise and see the truth for what it is. We must have conversations with them to understand and help them, instead of teaching them to listen, follow and obey.

However, my parents had different views about parenting and they never had conversations with me to get to know me. Our conversations were usually one way, and I was never given a chance to voice my opinion. They lived with their beliefs about me, which were baseless. I, on the other hand, got to know them better with each of their dealings with me. And through this, I felt that my parents would not support me if things went wrong in my life. *A parent who sees their girl as unworthy and incapable, and cares less about her life will never be there for her. A parent who lacks understanding and is failing to understand their child will always fail to understand them,* I told myself. I knew that I had to be my biggest support and make every decision with caution, to secure my life. I knew I was alone.

In many cultures, women are taken for granted, and people do not think it is important to consider a woman's feelings, likes, and dislikes. Women are not allowed to think for themselves, in many families and communities, since these communities believe a woman's life does not belong to her. As daughters, girls are taught to listen to their parents. Then parents get their daughters married off, after which these girls are supposed to listen to, and obey their husbands. Many communities believe that women are poor judges, so they cannot be given any power over their own lives, such as when choosing a life partner. So, parents make this decision for their daughters, caring little about what their daughters want or how they feel. This is a common practice in many parts of the world, even today.

When we think we know everything, and the other person knows nothing, this is ignorance at its best. The truth is, we misunderstand our belief as knowledge. When we take away the freedom of a fellow human, telling them they do not have a right to dream about their own lives, we deny them their basic human rights. Yet no one in these communities takes the time or trouble to start a conversation to correct such beliefs and injustices. Instead, women who go through such unfair practices, move on with their lives, unwilling to speak up. Starting a conversation on this topic would mean questioning what our own parents taught us and how they treated us, and many people feel that it is wrong to hurt the feelings of the people who raised us. But when we move on, without a word, these practices continue. Like all these women, I held back for years, but I have finally decided to share my experience and how it made me feel. Voicing my opinion about these practices is not about me or about my parents; it is about a wrong belief that has robbed many girls of their dreams and left them with tears for the rest of their lives. It is about correcting a deep-rooted practice that is hurting families, communities, and the world in many ways.

When women get forced into the practice of living against their wishes, they live lives filled with grief. When women are denied freedom, they feel worthless and miserable and something dies within them. When life dies within us, while we are still alive, what is left? Just the body? I know many women who drag their bodies around without life, like a zombie. People around them do not realize what these women are going through. They care less about women, all because they believe that is the right way to treat women—as second-class human beings.

If freedom is taken away from us, we feel suffocated since our flow towards our true purpose and desires is blocked. Freedom is the birthright of all living things, but human beings take away the freedom of others in the name of gender, race, religion and more. The world is mostly democratic, where every citizen is supposedly free. But are all humans free? In many parts of the world women are not free. Many societies believe that giving freedom to women is dangerous. They believe that if women are given freedom, they might live a life which can go against the wishes of the family and community. These communities believe in taking away the freedom of women, with an intention of protecting her. This belief is so strong, in many parts of the world that women themselves feel they have no right to freedom, since that is what they have witnessed for generations.

The truth is women are the most caring and creative section of the population. Given the freedom to express talent and creativity in life, women can not only help themselves but also help the people around them. Instead they are confined to roles that the family and society decides for them. When women are told they cannot dream or wish anything for themselves, that is the loss of freedom. When women are asked to listen and obey, by giving up what they truly want to be or do in life, that is denial of human rights. Generation after generation women are denied freedom and human rights in the name of gender. It is time we correct this practice.

We are trained to believe the world we live in and the environment that raised us. The world around us can hypnotize us to believe falsities about ourselves and others, by programming us to listen and obey others, and ignore our inner self. We end up living most, or all, our lives with these beliefs, until we face a crisis and overcome it. Only then do realize we got it all wrong. Only then do we realize our true potential.

We have far more potential than we think we do. However, we limit our potential due to our beliefs. When our families and societies teach us, we are inferior, why do we believe it? Why do we trust others more than we trust ourselves?

We believe a certain section of human beings are inferior, due to physical differences, and we think it is fair to discriminate. Why? Because we are following the footsteps of others before us, without thinking and reasoning. We are blindly believing those who taught us to discriminate, and we fail to act from a place of love and compassion. Discrimination can never arise from a place of love. It germinates from the soil of ego, fear, ignorance, and lack.

When a man discriminates against a woman, when one race discriminates against another, when the rich mistreat the poor, it comes from a place of ego and ignorance, and these actions feed the ego. The ego gives us temporary pleasure by making us feel superior. We misunderstand this feeling as true happiness and try to remain superior in the eyes of others. Little do we realize that we are using the wrong recipe to create happiness. Lasting Happiness or joy comes from a place within us, and not from the outside environment.

Few years back, I heard about a solitary shy animal that lives in mountain regions from Siberia to the Himalayas. It's called the musk deer since it produces the fragrant musk common in perfumes. Musk is extracted by killing the male deer, which carries extremely fragrant fluid secretion under its belly. When the deer secrets musk, it is attracted to the smell and tries to locate the source of the smell, by sticking its nose in rocks and thorns, getting hurt in the process. This poor animal is totally unaware that the source of the smell is in its own body and looks for it elsewhere. Human beings look for happiness the same way. Just like the musk deer, we are totally unaware that the source of our happiness is within each one of us, not outside of us. However, we look outside of us to find happiness. We are constantly trying to figure out what in the external world will make us happy. We fail to realize that the source of happiness is our own feelings and emotions, which arise from our thoughts. It is up to us to think and process our life experiences in ways that make us miserable, or choose to reflect on experiences positively, learned from it, and move on. It is absolutely ours to choose our thoughts and this decides our happiness.

A positive thought often results in positive feelings and emotions and it makes us happy. However, we focus less on our thoughts and emotions, and we react to situations around us all the time. We feel offended or became defensive too often and focus less on adopting a positive outlook. We hardly work on calming our minds, instead we expect the world around us to make us happy. It is ironic that the world is less interested in our happiness, and yet we believe that we should focus on the world to attain happiness. Where did this belief come from? Generation after generation, we have known that we cannot be happy if we live a life of people-pleasing, yet we follow the same path. Why?

It started when we were children - when we were taught to please others. We are labeled good when we please others and bad when we go against others in our environment. Soon, our feelings are impacted by how others treat us, and we focus on getting the people-pleasing right. We are not taught to focus on our emotions and make choices based on how we feel. Instead, the focus is on the emotions of others around us. So, looking outside for happiness soon becomes a habit, and we live with it for the rest of our lives. The truth is, if you are focused on others and ignore how you feel, you can never be happy.

Happiness is attained when we focus on our feeling and emotions, correct our beliefs, and see the reality around us as it is. We feel calm and at peace when we quiet our minds and shield ourselves from external noise. We do not need to please others or accumulate wealth for happiness. When we were born, we had nothing, but we were happy. Along the way, we accumulated many things, thinking they will make us happy. While things we own can make us temporarily happy, such happiness does not last.

Happiness is the greatest wealth on earth. The joy of life and living comes when you truly appreciate life and everything you see around you. For this, you must look at life positively and be grateful. But most of us are never content, instead, we always want more. To aspire for something better in life is natural, and there is nothing wrong with it. However, most of us want more to compare ourselves with people who have more, and comparison is the opposite of contentment. The more we get, the more we want. It is a never-ending cycle of "more," believing more will make us happy. Such people are far from happiness, since they fail to appreciate what life has offered them.

CHAPTER 4

YOUR INNER GURU WHO GUIDES YOU

I n my beautiful village most villagers lived below the poverty line. My friends in the neighborhood, who were poor, used to ask each other how much food they got for breakfast, like a normal conversation. They used to often warn each other, *"You are going to feel hungry soon, since you had less breakfast."*

Coming from a well-off family, I was shocked the first time I overheard this conversation. Knowing that my friends did not have enough to eat, like I did, made me feel sorry for them. Today, when I look back at these incidents, I see that while their stomachs might have been empty, their hearts were always full. I experienced over-flowing joy and contentment during my time with these kids. While I saw a lot of progress and wealth as I moved on in life, I never saw the kind of happiness and contentment in my life that I saw in this village during these years.

As I moved from village to town, I found that people in cities and towns were in the race to look better, have better, be better, and they ignored the simple things that bring joy in life. These people believed that money, power, and prestige brought happiness, and they willingly joined the rat race of competition and accumulation. The more people had, the more they focus on the external, material world with the belief that it will make them happy. When we do this, we ignore our inner voice and get lost in the external world. Most of us never hear the inner voice that is trying to guide us towards happiness, and there is a reason for this.

When you live in a noisy place, where your neighbor plays loud music all the time, will you be able to hear your mother calling you from the kitchen in a soft voice? That neighbor I am referring to, is your external environment, and the mother is the voice of life energy within you, or your inner voice. We fail to hear our inner voice when we are consumed by the external, materialistic world. Since we cannot hear our inner voice, we listen to the outer world, and we lose touch with our inner selves. We live our lives believing everything we see and hear outside of us, and we do not pay attention to our inner guidance.

Listening to our inner selves is key to happiness in life. Our lives' purpose is known by our inner being who gives us signals in the form of intuition, impulse, and passion, if we listen to ourselves. Sometimes it pushes us in a certain direction, gets us attached or interested in certain things, other times it comes as a strong impulse towards something. Often, these little signals of likes, dislikes, passion, etc. are ignored, and many of us confuse our lives' purpose as accumulating wealth and power.

Why do most people confuse life's purpose as accumulating wealth and fails to follow their impulse and intuitions? It is because of social programming and conditioning. As kids, we aspire to be something but later let go of that, since we believe, or are made to believe, that it is not right for us. We are programmed, in many ways, from the time we are born, to ignore the pulsating signal in us, and act according to the instructions of others. The purpose of our lives is wired into the core of our beings as a feeling of joy, love, passion, and enthusiasm. That signal always shows up as a positive, interesting, and exciting feeling within us. Unfortunately, we live in a world that believes that, just because some people are older, have lived longer, or are close to us, they know us better than we do, and should be the ones to decide how we live our lives. When these people convince us that our internal guidance system will not serve us, we stop listening to our inner guidance and we look for guidance from the external world.

The people around us cannot hear the inner voice in each of us, and they cannot feel the fire of desire in us. Only we can sense it. Any decision made by ignoring our internal guidance will not give us satisfaction. We get satisfaction when we are in sync with what we truly want to be or do in life. We need to bring out our true potential, not who others want us to be. We need to be entirely ourselves, living life fully. We experience joy when we are in sync with who we really are deep inside. When we are joyful, our bodies and minds function at their best, causing us to experience a profound sense of happiness. This is our desired state and the reason why people who follow their passion, live lives of joy, despite potentially having very little worldly wealth.

We are trained to find love and happiness outside of ourselves, and we are told that caring for what we want is selfish behavior. Self-love does not mean a lack of love for others; it means filling oneself with love so that it can be poured out to others around us. It means taking the path in life that will give us joy, so that we may spread joy in the world. Keeping ourselves in a place of joy is vital for both ourselves and others.

However, if the people around us are consumed by the material world and want something out of us, they will not want us to walk the path to finding happiness, instead they will be focused on what they want. If the path others want us to take, will make us unhappy, why do we choose that path? Why do we choose to be miserable to make others happy? Can someone who loves us be happy by taking away our happiness? How can the act of seeking happiness get us labelled as selfish? Isn't it selfish of others to ask us not to choose happiness?

As kids, we are taught to commit acts that leave others with a good impression of us. When others do not approve of us, we are labelled as a "bad" child. As a result, we grow up learning the importance of fitting in and people-pleasing. However, it is impossible to please everyone. If we let others determine what we should or should not be doing, we will soon make ourselves unhappy and miserable. Yet this is what most of us do.

People form opinions based on the little information they have about us. If we are going to allow the opinion of others, influence our thoughts and actions, we are ignoring our inner beings.

Each of us has our own inner guru, or conscience, that guides us through any given situation. Our emotions generate a feeling of well-being within us when we do good deeds. On the other hand, it tells us when we are wrong, by generating negative emotions like guilt. This is how our inner being communicates with us. However, if we refuse to listen to this guidance, I believe, the mechanism will shut itself down temporarily.

As an example, when we choose to be dishonest for the very first time, we feel a strong sense of guilt. If we ignore this feeling and act dishonestly for a second time, we still feel guilty for our action, but not as strongly this time. As we continue to take this wrong path by ignoring the inner guidance, we will feel less and less guilty every subsequent time. At a certain point, we will lose the inner guidance due to our refusal to listen to it, and we end up walking the wrong path.

Our inner guru is like a good parent, correcting a child. A good parent takes the time and trouble to tell us when we do something wrong. If we refuse to listen, and continue with the bad behavior, by the second or third time, the parent may still offer corrections, but they now know, that we are not planning to listen. At this point, the parent may try to find another way to correct us. Often it is through punishment, to bring us back on track. Just like our parents, our inner guidance will eventually stop reacting, if neglected, and sooner or later we will face a negative or painful experience, that will force us to realize the consequences of our actions. This is karma—a way by which our inner guidance brings us back on track when we do not listen to our conscience.

In some societies, the lack of emotions is looked upon as strength. "Don't cry, be a man," is a common adage many have heard. People who cry easily, or who are full of empathy and kindness, are perceived as weak. Empathy is a sense of our soul. The lack of kindness, compassion, and empathy means that we are disconnected from our inner beings or true selves. A person with empathy can sense the deep connection to their true self and the world around them. Emotions like compassion and empathy are the energy that connect us to the world around us. If our skin helps us to sense the material world, our emotions help us sense the non-material world. Empathy helps us understand and sense the emotions of other beings and the connection we all have as inhabitants of this planet. Being aware of others and what they are feeling, is a strength, not a weakness. An emotional being is a conscience being, who is more aware of their surroundings. Such a being can see things clearly because they can sense everything around them. Emotions come with an awareness that we are all connected to each other, and we all belong together. When people lack emotions, my experience has found that they also lack awareness. They see themselves as separate or isolated from the rest and cannot feel or empathize with others around them. If we did not have skin on our bodies, we would not be able to sense anything. Similarly, the lack of emotions is like absence of our awareness and ability to sense what others are experiencing. We need this awareness to know the world around us. Just like the five senses of our physical bodies, emotions such as kindness and empathy are crucial senses to the conscience within each of us. They are non-physical senses of our inner being that guides us in the right direction.

Our mind and our conscience are different, and it is easy to confuse the two. Our conscience is our inner being—the part of us that is connected to the source of all creation. The mind contains the noise in your head like the noisy world outside. That noise is the little monkey on your back, jumping around and feeding you back-to-back thoughts and creating ongoing mental chatter. It makes us restless by feeding us thoughts about unpleasant events, and it constantly keeps our minds busy. The mind is restless like a monkey, and it needs to be trained and tamed, for us to get in touch with our inner being or conscience.

Meditation is a method of training our mind, to stop the ongoing flow of thoughts, to raise awareness and get us in touch with our inner being. Meditation forces the mind to be still, and that stillness opens a window to our inner being. Calming our minds gives us access to our inner selves. Meditation is a simple technique of sitting down with our eyes closed and focusing on one thing. It can be a steady sound or the light you see in your third eye. You may also use your breath, or anything that is generating a steady sound, and feel comfortable focusing. The point is to block all thoughts with a single steady focus. People who have difficulty meditating with eyes closed can meditate with the eyes open, staring at the wonders of nature, like a tree or the sky, feeling the peace within and experiencing the joy of creation. Peace gradually overcomes those who continue the practice of meditation. As the practice continues the person starts to experience a constant state of inner peace and joy. Slowly but surely, our intuitions will start working more effectively, and we will see a shift in our experiences.

Once we are in touch with this inner conscience, it will guide our actions through our feelings and emotions. Feelings and emotions are the tools each of our inner beings use to communicate with us and take us in the right direction. Often, we experience synchronicities and coincidences when we get into the practice of meditation. Pay attention to these since these are divine guidance. We must choose to focus on our emotions and let our inner beings guide us. Be aware of the world around us and use empathy and compassion to connect with others. Sense the world around us, not just with the five senses of our physical bodies, but with the senses rooted in our feelings and emotions. We must always watch our emotions and focus on how they guide us through life.

We must live lives guided by our inner beings and keep the ego-centric mind in check. We need to pay attention to how things make us feel, and not what others will think or say. What people say is no more than their opinion, and opinions can be accurate or inaccurate. People have the right to their opinions, but that does not mean they are right, so we must learn to differentiate between fact and opinion. There is a power within each one of us, our focus should be on this power within us. If we harness our inner strength, we can live a loving and happy life and pour out, love and joy into this world.

CHAPTER 5

FINDING HAPPINESS

When I look back at my life, the most beautiful years were the years I spent in my village. With little to live with, the people in my village lived very happy lives, and there was peace and contentment in every family, at that time. As time progressed, things changed. People left the villages to find jobs in the middle east. In most families, at least one family member worked in the middle east. Neighbors who used to live with love for each other, slowly started to develop competition as money flowed in from the middle east.

Money made the people shift their focus in life. People started measuring and respecting each other based on their financial status. My village and villagers were undergoing a transformation, all because of the influx of money. Most people saw this as progress, but the village was losing something—the joy of life and living.

When people focus on the external world and let the external world influence their thoughts and actions, we lose control of our happiness and the world controls our happiness for us. To be happy, and remain in that happy state, we need to take the focus completely off the external world, focusing on our internal world, of our thoughts, feelings, and emotions. There will be times when life knocks us down—that is the nature of life. However, we often knock ourselves down, simply by our thoughts, far more often than what life does.

We all live in two worlds: the material world, and the world of illusion that our minds create for us. Often, we are so lost in the mind's illusion that we hardly notice the reality surrounding us. Our ability to overcome our mind's thoughts, shutting off the mental chatter, is a key factor in achieving happiness.

How does our mind work? Most of the time, our minds focus on unpleasant things. If we catch ourselves having a negative or unpleasant thought, we must choose to focus on another, more pleasant thought. Taming the mind is like taming an animal, and our minds will not easily give up control. Get into the habit of replacing every negative thought with a positive one. Like everything else in life, changing our thoughts comes with practice. The mind will keep returning to old, established thought patterns, resisting change. But as we continue to practice, focusing on positive thoughts will become a habit, and the mind will begin to feed us good thoughts rather than negative ones.

Happiness is an internal state of being. It is not something we can achieve with external factors like money and material goods, these can only give us temporary happiness. Happiness is a habit each of us can cultivate within ourselves by thinking right and focusing on positive emotions. When we help the poor, we feel profound happiness. When we make a difference in someone's life, we feel an internal shift and feel good about ourselves. Yet many people choose to accumulate wealth by hurting others, believing that wealth and power will make them happy. Most of the world is unaware of the key that unlocks the world of happiness within us. The key to happiness is our emotion. Generate the right emotion in you by listening to your inner guidance or the divine in you - this is the simple truth about happiness. Nothing else can get you this treasure – no amount of money can buy it; no power can hand it to you.

I recently had an accident where I severely fractured my right leg. I was bedridden for almost five months. Though I was always grateful for most of the things in life, I had never reflected on the importance of good health and a fully functional, healthy body until that point in time. It was during those five months that I realized how grateful I should have been for having two working legs and a healthy body. It had never occurred to me, until then, how difficult it is when one leg stops functioning. That accident opened my eyes and taught me to be more grateful. I was grateful to be able to breathe without a machine, eat without a tube, taste wonderful food, hear the sweet voices, see the beauty of everything around me . . . I could go on and on. But the truth is that most of us take these things for granted. We breathe every second without even realizing we are breathing. We ignore this profound mechanism until the day we need a machine to help us breathe. Only then do we look back and see the power of our breath. We never focus on these profound mechanisms that god have gifted us, why? We are too busy to reflect on all these things, and we take it for granted.

If we had gratitude for everything around us, for how it is serving us, we would live our lives very differently from how we are living today. Instead, we focus on using everything around us for our external comfort, and we lack gratitude for nature and everything in it. If we see the wonders of creation and the creator, and see how important they are for our survival, we will live our lives with more gratitude. However, this power- and wealth-centric era of humanity is so short sighted. We only focus on ourselves and short-term gains. We perceive everything on the planet as separate from us and fail to see the connection. Because of this we cause harm to anyone or anything by believing that everything is under our control. We forget that we do not have control over everything; we don't even know what will happen to us in the next minute, or if we will live to see the next day. We have no control over tomorrow, or the time we have on this planet, but we live our lives like we are going to live forever. We accumulate wealth and try to control everything, like we are running this planet and the planet cannot survive without us. The truth is, this planet can and will survive without us, but we cannot live without this planet. It is high time we realize this truth. Nature can uproot anything that exists in it, making it extinct. We push the limits, and yet nature is so kind to us. Dinosaurs and so many other living beings have perished from this planet. Can human beings stop such a major disaster from hitting us? To some extent we can, by respecting nature and by ceasing to abuse the planet.

If we can live our lives with gratitude, knowing that everything around us is a wonder, profound happiness will run through us. The grand nature of the universe will slowly unfold in our thoughts and feelings, and we will feel blessed for being a part of the wonder. If we choose to live life knowing that all life is divine, it will bring a total shift in us. Wonder at the beauty of creation, observe it, and notice its unique nature, watch how you feel inside. It will fill you with joy and peace. Respect nature and know that a tree is not just a collection of shoots, roots, and leaves, but a living being that is much more rooted in this planet than we are. A tree can feel the planet as part of its being; it is connected to earth through its roots and to the environment through its surface area. Sitting or walking in places full of trees makes us happier. We wonder at them, enjoy the shade and the fresh air, rest under them, and experience happiness when we are around them. In nature, we can listen to the chirping of the birds and wind blowing the trees, and we can feel how wonderful it is. If we indulge in nature; appreciate nature; and live life with love, appreciation, and gratitude, we will see how much joy it can bring us.

Happiness is a practice of seeing life with gratitude and seeing every living being with respect and with wonder. We must be good, do good, and live lives filled with loving intention. If we can do this, happiness will flow to us like a never-ending stream.

CHAPTER 6

LISTEN TO YOUR INNER VOICE,
NOT YOUR FEARS

The Nair community, in southern India—the community I was born into, treated women with respect. Historically, Nair was a community of warriors and royals. Nair kings would crown their sisters' sons, their nephews, as their successors instead of their sons. Family wealth was passed from mother to daughter, and after marriage, daughters would live in their parents' homes, as per community tradition. Property was passed on through women in the family, and mothers and daughters lived under one roof, supporting each other, because the Nair men were warriors and led dangerous and uncertain lives. This tradition ensured that women and children were taken care of, under all circumstances, and the practice gave women a respectable place in the family and society. As time went by, most of these traditions changed, with people moving out of the joint-family system in search of jobs.

Ancient Indian Vedic era was a time when women were treated with great respect. After the Vedic era, the country underwent many changes. It also changed the outlook on women in many parts of the country.

People who believed that women were weak choose to treat their sons one way, and their daughters another. Girls were labelled as not good enough, without taking notice of their capabilities.

This practice instilled the belief that boys are an assets and girls are a responsibility. Boys are looked upon as gifted beings to whom fathers should pass the baton, while girls are disregarded in some communities. Growing up, I watched girls in some families around me being forced to make choices based on what their parents wanted. These "choices" included major life decisions, such as giving up education and stepping into marriage. Some parents felt that marriage was a way of ending the responsibility they have toward their daughter. Through marriage, she would become someone else's responsibility. This attitude interested me, because I could not understand how any parent could wash their hands of their daughter. I also found it baseless, because these girls had immense talents, and if given an education and opportunity, they could achieve profound success. Regardless, all what most parents cared about, when it came to their daughters, was marriage. Their daughters' happiness, or how their lives would turn out, seemed less important to parents. They simply refused to think about it.

Many incidents made it clear to me that my father was among the parents who held this mindset toward girls. He believed I was a responsibility that he needed to get married off. This hurt me deeply and instilled in me the feeling that I did not belong in my home. One example involved my passion for dance. I was drawn to dance from the first time I saw a performance at two or three years old. I loved it so much that every time I saw a performance, my eyes would be glued to the dancers, and I would come home and imitate the performance, and my maternal family, watched my little performance with love. I would constantly ask my parents to send me to dance classes, but no matter how many times I asked, my parents refused. One day, I overheard my father tell my mother, *"She is a girl. We must get her married anyway. Why should we spend any more money on her?"* I was shocked. My parents did not realize I had overheard their conversation, and they never told me this directly. My father felt spending money on a girl was a waste, and it was not because he did not have the money; he just saw girls differently.

Girls were denied opportunities and a voice, in many families, and they were considered unfit for anything but marriage. Some societies even mourn the birth of a female child. Why do each generation fall into such blind beliefs when there are examples all over the world to disprove it? Why do people refuse to see the truth? Girls that receive the opportunity succeed in life however, the few women who get that opportunity are labelled as different than other women. The truth is all what made the difference is the opportunity that these successful women received. The opportunities they received helped them succeed. However, this truth was often rejected.

I experienced the pain of this belief system in my family, with my own parents. I tried my best to show them that there were successful women and that I could be one of them. No matter how much I tried, they were unwilling to change their opinion about girls, or me. What was even more surprising to me, was that in the Nair community I hail from, hardly anyone thought this way. How did my parents pick up this belief?

My father decided that I would be married young, without first giving me a proper education. He wanted a marriage that will lift his social status and prestige; that was his only focus in finding me a husband. All he wanted was for a rich, reputable man to marry me, to boost his reputation. He was clear about what he wanted and never cared about what I wanted.

Why do parents think more about their reputation and less about their child's happiness and future? Ego feels the need to be superior and losing superiority drives fear into people. Being at the top of the social hierarchy and looking good in the eyes of others is more important in life, than anything else, for egocentric minds. This ego-based fear is what causes people to blindly follow beliefs, without love and compassion. The ego, and the actions fueled by ego, drives us to safeguard our reputation, often ignoring the wellbeing of others, even our own children. Many social and religious practices that do not make sense are driven by the fear generated by ego. People fear that things can go wrong if we refuse to follow tradition. They fail to think if the tradition makes sense, and fear breaking the old patterns. They feel it safer to stick to the old cycle of beliefs and practices. In my case, my father believed in the practice of getting girls married off early which safeguards reputation. He did not see a reason why he should give me an opportunity in life to fulfill my dreams. He believed it was my lack of understanding, that is driving me towards a dream, which he believed I was not capable of achieving.

People who blindly practice rules and traditions, fear going against practices established years before by their previous generations. They feel comfortable sticking to old practices and fear the unknown. Fearing the unknown and refusing to think, question and reason existing practices, is the major cause of many issues we see today. Violence based on issues of gender, religion, and race, for example, comes from a place of fear, ignorance, and lack of understanding. Many people believe that those who look different are a threat, but if we are willing to see the truth, we know that this is a false belief planted in the mind through years of conditioning. If we are willing to think, question and reason with an open mind, our ignorance and lack of understanding will be replaced with clarity, and our fears will be washed away.

Discrimination is strongly rooted in false beliefs and ego. Following the thoughts and ideas of those before us, with a failure to think clearly can be toxic. It not only forces people to act without love and compassion, but also hurt fellow humans without a good realization of the wrong actions. All discrimination grows from the same soil of ignorance and fear, becoming a catalyst for creating division among people.

Some people are not comfortable with differences, be it skin color, religion, or gender. We make up narratives about those who look or live differently than us, and most of the narratives we believe about the "other" is our imagination. We believe we are right about the others, and we never doubt for once, that we could be wrong. We accept the beliefs and narratives we have created about others as truth. And when these narratives create a fear of the "other," we feel the need to protect ourselves, often through violence.

If on the other hand, we accept the simple truth that we all look different and live a little differently, but that we are more alike than we are different, this fear will be washed away. We must, for once, look at our differences and try to understand the purpose behind them. What is the difference between men and women? There are few differences like some body parts, hormones etc.; however, as humans we are mostly alike. We are more alike than different, yet we only focus on the differences. What is the difference between various races of the world? Each race looks a little different from the other, and they have certain sets of beliefs, practices, and way of living. Other than these things, there is not much difference. We all experience the same emotions and have the same needs. But we do not focus on the similarities; we always go by the external differences, which causes us to fear the other.

If we look closely, we can see that violence, injustice, fear, ignorance, and a lack of understanding exist where we magnify our differences. Wars are fought out of fear or the need for power and control. Losing power and control causes fear in the egocentric mind. When we have no fear, we do not look for power. Where there is ego, there is always a need to accumulate power. Ego fears losing power. When we are not in the grip of our ego, we are filled with love and compassion instead of fear. Fear is the seed that germinates into various negative emotions in all of us. It causes stress in our daily lives; it makes us feel threatened and dislike others; it makes us fight wars against countries, races, religions, and much more. Yet fear remains hidden in all our hearts, disguised, covering its ugly face, and making us believe the "other" is the cause of all our problems. And by failing to recognize this negative energy, we let it grow within us.

People who have achieved success have overcome fear. Malala Yousafzai, the brave young lady from the Swat district of Pakistan, and her parents, are one such example. Malala's father spoke in an interview with Oprah Winfrey[1] about how he raised Malala. He said something so profound it touched my heart. He mentioned that, where he comes from, most fathers believe that loving their daughters meant taking away their freedom, with an intention of protecting them. He explained that his definition of love was freedom, and he let his daughter, Malala, experience freedom from a very young age. He said that giving her a voice and the right to an opinion, was what he did differently with Malala, compared to the families around him.

What made him do this? It was the understanding that a girl is no different than a boy when it comes to her abilities as a human being. This father refused to give in to the fear of what people around him would think or how they would react. He understood that the true essence of his daughter, did not lie in her gender, but at the core of her being. The courage and understanding in this father gifted this world with a wonderful and brave woman named Malala, who set to make the world a better place.

What happens when parents fear? When parents fear, they think more about what people around them think and less about the lives of their own children. They buy into the society's beliefs and condition their children in keeping with those beliefs. My parents were among the many who bought into such beliefs. My outspoken character was not positively perceived, and they would constantly tell me to hold back and not to voice my opinion. Since, until the age of seven, I was raised in a joint-family system with people who thought very differently than my parents, my parents failed in convincing me that I was less capable. The joint family in which I grew up gave me such a boost of self-esteem that it lasted long enough to help me achieve my dreams.

At age seventeen, while still in high school, I received my first wedding proposal. It happened when a man came home to meet my father and noticed me. He knew someone who was looking for a young girl to marry. I overheard my parents' conversation and was shocked to hear the disappointment. I was still in school and hardly seventeen—not even the legal age for marriage. I was scared and cried continuously after overhearing the discussions. I felt my parents did not care about me and were trying to get rid of me. I wished I could run away and take care of myself, but I had no money or education, I was too young. I was overwhelmed with fear. Seeing how scared and upset I was, my mother spoke to my father, and that was the end of the marriage discussion, for the time.

Across the world, there are enough successful women to prove that girls can do whatever men can. They can manage careers and financial responsibility. So why do educated people still have such a mindset toward girls? When people become followers and lack the ability to think independently, they live their lives in ignorance. They seek social status and lack the ability to ask basic questions. But every parent must ask some basic questions, such as:

- How will this decision impact my child's future?

- Will my child be truly happy?

- Will my actions give my child happiness and security, or am I doing it to conform to a social norm?

While not many people are willing to ask these questions, doing so and reflecting on the answers will guide the parents to help their children in the right ways.

I often tried to make my parents understand the dangers of entering a marriage without an education. Placing my life, and the life of my future kids, in the hands of a man whom I do not even know felt like a huge risk to me. Arranged marriage, which my society practiced, gives little room to get to know your betrothed before marriage. To make my parents think, I would ask them questions like:

- What if my husband turns out to be an alcoholic and beats me and my kids?

- What if my husband dies young and I have no money to raise my kids?

- What will I do and where will I go, without a job or money?

Despite my efforts, my parents did not care to think, or answer my questions. My father said I was foolish and lacked understanding, the reason I was asking these questions. Some people told me, "*That's the way it is. Everyone goes through it. Why are you complaining?*" Others tried explaining that if bad things were to happen, that would be a result of my bad luck or destiny.

The truth is, there is a lot that can be done to stop this cycle. If girls are educated and independent, she can take care of herself and financially support her kids. I tried explaining to my parents that the practice was neither right nor destiny, but the blind following of tradition without thinking or caring about the girls involved. Just because girls have been treated this way for ages, does not make it right. Girls who ended up in unfortunate situations struggled to take care of their innocent children; they had no financial help.

They struggled to feed and shelter their children. Many examples of such girls existed all around, but no one was interested in noticing or understanding the problem. Many young women and children ended up helpless and homeless in the face of losing their husband/ father through death or divorce. However, this is never addressed, and people were less sensitive to such issues. The unfortunate circumstances are always perceived as destiny, and the practice continued without compassion, love and empathy towards girls and women who were facing such issues.

My grandmother was one of the few people, who saw the potential danger of such a practice. She educated all her daughters and delayed their marriages until they completed their education and got a job. She once told me, "*The reason I educated my girls is because they should be able to support themselves if unfortunate things happen. They should be equipped with an education, to find a job if needed, because in life, things can go wrong. If something happens, I don't want to see my children and grandchildren suffer.*" She made sure her daughters were educated and could support themselves if necessary. She educated them during a time when all the girls in the village were married off in their teenage years, without an education. My grandparents had to fight their society to get their daughters educated; people used to belittle them for sending girls to college in a time when women were confined to home. But with my grandfather's support, my grandmother cared more about her daughters and less about what people had to say. Some people in the village used to intentionally hurt my grandparents by saying they are educating their daughters to make money out of them. Hearing such comments was very painful for my grandparents, who were otherwise reputable in the village. But such criticism did not discourage them from educating their daughters.

What made my grandmother stand strong in her belief to educate her daughters was her own life experience. As a child, I noticed my grandmother was angry quite often, and her anger had a source of deep pain. Only later did I learn the source of my grandmother's pain. My grandmother was a brilliant student and had a passion for learning and she dreamed of a career. She had a loving father who was willing to let her fulfil her dreams. My great grandfather - her father, was a jail warden, and the family lived near his workplace - the central jail. Her father supported her and encouraged her, which was unusual during that time, when families all around them saw girls only as a marriage material. After her seventh-grade schooling, during her school holidays, she went to visit the joint-family members with her father. During this visit, a key member of the extended family strongly spoke out against educating my grandmother. The men in the extended family claimed educating a girl is wrong. My great grandfather could not go against these highly respected family members.

Unable to tell his daughter not to go to school, my great grandfather stayed with the joint family until the day my grandmother's school reopened. Seeing that her father wasn't leaving, and knowing she needed to be back to school the next day, my grandmother asked her father, *"Father, don't you think we should leave? My school is reopening tomorrow."* With tears in his eyes, my great grandfather told my grandmother, *"My child, I am sorry. Please don't go to school again."* My grandmother controlled her tears because she saw her father's pain. She did not want her father to get hurt, but this caused her immense pain.

She stopped going to school for her father, but she could not resist her passion to learn. She was asked not to go to school anymore, but she could still learn. With her father's permission, she found another way to learn. She took her writing materials and went to the jail with her father. While he was on duty at the jail, she would ask the prisoners of the jail to teach her. These prisoners came from various places all over the country, and they knew different languages. She asked them to teach her their native languages, and they gladly did.

Every day she went along with her father, and the jail became her new school.

Six months later, the very same people who had robbed her of education came to my great grandfather again. This time they asked for her to get married to my grandfather. By that time, she had learned to read and write in six different languages. My grandmother was married at thirteen years old, and neither her nor her father had any say in it. I have heard that, in those days, most people in Indian communities would not question the elders in their families – it was considered disrespectful and bad behavior. Like my great grandfather, with a heavy heart, they would obey.

My grandmother was one of the most efficient women I have ever met. She was gifted in many ways. She had talent, strength, intelligence, and skill at decision making. She had huge potential, but her abilities never saw the light of the day, because her society programmed her to fail. Her crushed dreams made her bitter, and this bitterness came out when discussing the topic of women and girls. She would boil up inside, time and again, when it came to these conversations. Seeing her abilities, my grandfather left most of the familial and financial decisions to her, and she did a great job at everything she undertook. She loved her family, but she was never truly happy. She had been robbed of her smile.

Even though times have changed, girls around the world are still denied education and forced into marriage. Girls who have been through such situations have always taken it in silence. But the silence of all the girls who have walked this path has contributed to the issue, and people now see it as normal. I cannot be quiet and contribute to this problem; I need to voice my opinion about such practices, so that we can correct it and make this world a better place for younger generation.

As a young adult, I was scared that I would end up giving up my dreams due to this infinite cycle of wrong beliefs. The fear opened my eyes to reality and gave me the energy to fight against all obstacles that stood my way. But I know a lot of girls who, unlike me, trusted the system. Why did they do that?

We idealize our parents and believe that they cannot make mistakes when it comes to what is best for us. Parents mean everything to most of us. If parents can never be wrong, and we have a desire that goes against our parents' beliefs, we start doubting ourselves. This self-doubt makes young girls give up their dreams and follow what their parents have in mind for them. I was fortunate in that I never doubted my inner self. I believed that a girl is a human being, just like a boy, and no one has the right to take my rights away from me for being a girl. I have the right to be happy, and I will find happiness my own way, by never giving up my dreams to please someone else. That way is by blazing a new trail, with courage, and by cutting down obstacles of outdated beliefs and practices. When people told me that I was not smart enough to succeed, I told them they were wrong about me. I had the courage to face those who believed I was not good enough; I feared no one and spoke when I felt it was necessary.

Each person is unique in how they think, and I thought differently from the girls around me. Some communities around the world do not believe in giving girls their freedom. They believe girls should grow up to be obedient daughters and obedient wives. They want girls to live in silence, never raising their voices. They believe it is unnecessary to care about what a girl wants and how she feels. Both her parents and her husband can take her for granted because they believe she is lesser in all aspects of life.

When a society is consumed with such beliefs, human rights perish. Looking back, I am glad that I fought for my rights, but most girls lacked the courage to do the same. Some of these girls could have achieved a lot in life, if they were given the education they rightly deserved. Their lives would have been brighter, and their lights would have brightened the lives of others around them. But instead their lights were blown out through this series of beliefs and practices that did not serve them, all because they were born as feminine gender.

Why do we make it such a big deal and discriminate fellow humans based on gender? What is gender? Gender determines the way we look physically, however, we all feel the same in our spirit. I am not only a body but also a pure life energy. I choose to think and act in ways that feel right to me as a being. I am more than my body; I am a being full of energy. My energy is not tied to specific gender. It is the body that gives me gender. But most of the world is oblivious to the energy within our bodies, identifying us by our bodies more than anything else. Are we just this body? If this body is all that I am then what is the difference between my living and dead body? The difference is the energy we call life. When I am alive, my energy nourishes my body. When my energy departs my physical body, then my body is dead, but my energy lives on. Gender is mother nature's way of sustaining species by creating both the male and female for reproduction, keeping the balance of creation. There is nothing more to gender than this in my opinion. But not many like to see the truth.

One day while I was in high school studying for my exams, a young man my father knew came rushing to our home to deliver a package. As he rushed back to his car, my father asked him why he was in such a hurry. Joyfully, the man replied, *"I just got a call that my wife has delivered our first baby; I am going to the hospital to see them!"*

Hearing the news, my father congratulated the man, paused, and then asked, *"Boy or girl?"*

"Girl," the man replied.

"Oh . . . don't worry," my father responded as the man walked to his car and drove away.

My father's response was spontaneous and unintentional, but it shocked me. I could imagine how it would have made the man feel. I watched the joy and excitement leave his face at my father's response, and I felt sorry for the young man and his daughter. I knew that one response had the power to change the way the man thought about his newborn daughter. The man had a lot of respect for my father, and my father's opinion would be influential over his views. My father had the power to rewrite the relationship between that father and daughter, even before that young man had seen her.

Opportunities, and how they are seized, is what makes children successful, irrespective of gender. If we snatch opportunities away from girls, we program girls a failure, which perpetuates the idea that they are less worthy and capable; this is unfair. People talk of women empowerment, but I do not think it is a question of empowerment. If we stop depriving women and girls of their freedom and human rights, that will solve the issue. If we let young girls grow the same way we allow their male counterparts, if we grant girls choice and opportunity, if we put an end to gender discrimination, that will reverse the need for female empowerment. Do not treat her as less worthy; see her as human.

Consider two birds. One bird we let fly, and we admire its wings. We clip the other bird's wings and throw it in the air, but it falls. Empowering this second bird will not make it fly; we have made sure of that. This is the story of women and woman empowerment. Girls around the world who faced discrimination growing up, are like birds without wings. Society had clipped her wings and then labeled her as weak. But if we give women their birth right of freedom, women will prosper. And when women prosper, societies and communities will prosper. We must treat everyone with love and respect and remove the blindfold of race, gender, and religion. We must stop judging people by their external appearance and stop letting people treat us as less worthy. We cannot waste our lives being the victims of beliefs and practices.

"Your time is limited, so don't waste it living someone else's life. Don't be trapped by dogma – which is living with the results of other people's thinking. Don't let the noise of others' opinions drown out your own inner voice. And most important, have the courage to follow your heart and intuitions. They somehow already know what you truly want to become. Everything else is secondary."[2]

-Steve Jobs.

CHAPTER 7

FEAR AND CONTROL

Human beings have a wonderful ability to think and reason unlike any other living being in nature. Unfortunately, we tend to use these skills not only to help ourselves but also to generate fear and stress. How many times in a day do we experience fear? If we reflect on this, we will see how much this negative emotion has become part of our daily lives. We live with a constant worry that things will go wrong, and they rarely do. This strategy of thinking might have protected the primitive human beings, who needed to constantly be on the lookout for danger to survive. We live in a different environment now, but the fear and our internal mechanism works the same way it did back then. When we experience fear and worry by thinking that things will go wrong, we end up stressed.

What would happen if we forced ourselves to trust that everything will work out just fine? If we develop this positive attitude, we will have a better day, even if things do go wrong. If we carry on our days with a positive belief, our days will be better simply because we stopped worrying. If we can be aware of our thoughts and practice having a positive outlook, our better days will lead to living a better life. We must start seeing life for the bigger picture and stop worrying about the small mistakes we make. We are not born to be perfect, so we cannot expect perfection from ourselves or anybody else. Instead, we must use these errors as learning experiences and do, or be, better next time.

Fear is not always a bad thing, if used the right way. Fear can ignite our inner drive and should work as a reminder for us to do well and be better. People should use fear the same way as every other living being in nature uses it—to protect itself. However, fear often paralyzes us, doing more harm than good, so it is important that we learn to handle fear.

When fear is at the wheel, it negatively impacts both our lives and the lives of those around us. Fear often blocks our view when it comes to major life decisions. We fear how others will perceive us if we break the old ways of doing things. We steer children to follow our thoughts and outdated practices because of fear. We stand in opposition to our children's dreams, believing we know what is best for them. When we do this, we fail to realize the impact it has on them. We change the course of our children's lives when we force them to take the path, we want them to take. Often these actions and decisions we make stems from fear. The dream the child carries in their heart is their path to joy. When a child's dream is destroyed, their life's happiness and the love they feel for the person standing in their way vanishes in most cases. They cannot open their mind, with love, to a person who forced them to abandon their dreams. But when we open our hearts, see a child's dream, and let them fulfil their dreams, the love they feel for the person standing by them is profound. We can only do this if we let go of our fears.

Rethinking and correcting our thoughts and beliefs is like cleaning our lives of clutter that no longer serves us. We take the trouble to clean our house. Isn't it even more important to reflect on our lives and do a clean-up of our thoughts and beliefs?

I lived my life, for the most part, with a lot of fear. Fear of losing my freedom and having my life decided for me. With my freedom and dreams taken away from me, I knew my life would be miserable. I am glad I had the courage to fight for want I wanted in life. I am grateful for having a mind of my own, which helped me think differently from the girls around me growing up. I want girls to realize how important it is to express their opinion and demand freedom of choice without fear, especially when it comes to their own lives. I want parents to know that daughters can make a difference in their lives, just like their sons can. Girls can fly high if their wings are not clipped. We must give them the freedom to fly and watch them reach heights we never imagined they could. The simple act of letting girls be who they are can change their life's outcome and positively influence the people around them. If given the opportunity to succeed, women will give back to the families and communities who contributed to their success.

From my experience, and the experiences of many other girls all over the world, I am reminded of a story my great grandmother told me as a child. It was about the Hindu God Hanuman. Hanuman had superpowers that no one could beat. He was like a superhero. He had super strength, could fly, could grow, and shrink to any size within seconds, and so much more. Hanuman was He-Man, Superman, and Batman all rolled into one. But he was completely unaware of his strength for a long time. As a little boy, Hanuman playfully misused his strength to cause mischief that upset many of the saints, disturbed them during their prayers and meditations. One day, tired of his mischief, a saint cursed him- that he will forget his superpower. Hanuman slowly began to forget his physical strength and extraordinary abilities. The strong Hanuman went on to live an ordinary life, not knowing of his powers. Years later, Hanuman was part of a search-and-rescue operation for King Rama. Queen Sita, the wife of King Rama, had been abducted by the king of Sri Lanka and taken there. Those who knew Hanuman's real strength, asked him to cross the ocean to Sri Lanka, and Hanuman was shocked by the request. He did not know he was capable of such a task. Believing he could not cross the ocean to Sri Lanka, he did not understand how people could ask him to complete such an impossible task. Seeing what Hanuman was going through, one of the wise ones in the army, named Jambavan, started praising Hanuman and reminding him of his strength. He reminded Hanuman of all the mischievous things he had done when he was a child, and the reason why he forgot his own strength. He kept praising him until Hanuman felt confident enough to accomplish the task at hand. With vigor and a new-found confidence, Hanuman crossed the ocean, found Queen Sita, and flew back to give King Rama the news. In the battle that followed between the two mighty kings, Hanuman acted as a real superhero. And with his help, Queen Sita was reunited with her husband.

The beliefs of women in many parts of the world are like the story of Hanuman. Women have been conditioned to forget what they are capable of. Women have forgotten their powers, just like Hanuman forgot his. We need a wake-up call to know what we can really achieve. We are told and taught that we are incapable, or that we are not good enough, but the belief that we are not good enough is dangerous, and most of us carry it all our lives. If we believe we are not good enough, we will never succeed. When families tell girls, they are not good enough, the belief programs girls for failure. If we let that program run us, it will destroy us, and we are sure to fail. We must know our strength and understand that we can achieve success. We can achieve anything in life if we believe in ourselves.

When we are told we cannot succeed, we refuse to try because we believe we will fail. What if the only reason we fail in life is because we refused to try? Trying and failing is better than failing because we refused to try. If I refused to try, I would have failed in my life. I would have never received an education or have written this book. I am glad I chose to try, and not believe the narrative I was told about being a girl. My question is, are you willing to try?

CHAPTER 8

THE POWER OF FORGIVENESS
AND GRATITUDE

I feel fortunate to have been born into a joint-family system where people valued education. I grew up among strong independent women in the family and that gave me the courage and confidence to be independent. However, there were few people in the family and community that discouraged girls from choosing an independent life. In this community when few believed that girls are just a responsibility, others challenged these beliefs, which proved to be a blessing for me.

The neighborhood I grew up in during my teenage years, was full of girls, some of these girls were my age. Most of them had parents who were obsessed with educating their children and wanted them to do well in life. These parents did not discriminate against their kids and saw their daughters as equal to their sons. One of the girls who was my age, went to the same school as me, and we shared many classes. Her parents wanted her to do well in school and were unhappy when she would score low in class. When test results would come out, to please her parents and get out of any trouble for scoring low, she would tell them, *"Priya scored poorly in the class—worse than me."* I was a far better student but telling this lie that compared our grades would shield her from trouble. In neighborhood chit-chat, her parents would brag about how their daughter scored more than me, to convey to everyone that their daughter was smarter. When this gossip related to my grades and academic performance reached my parents, they got extremely angry with this family for spreading false news about me. The gossip created competition between both these families when it came to the education of their daughters. This neighbor would go above and beyond to have their daughter educated, which forced my father to give in to the same competitive mode regarding my education. These small lies the girl told about me, triggered this change in my father and turned out to be a blessing in disguise for me.

I noticed this incident changed my parent's views about educating me, and they stopped the discussion of my marriage and started talking about my education. With the help and support of my parents I continued my education. The change in my parent's outlook towards me and my education brought me such joy, and I felt secure for the first time in my life. I got into a good university in India and was happy and dreamed of a wonderful future.

However, before I could complete my education my father asked me to drop out, and enter a marriage, they had decided for me. It made me realize that my parents had sent me to college for the sake of their own reputation, and they never cared about what I wanted. They were back on their original plan of getting me married. The man they found for me fit all my father's criteria for social prestige. He worked as an engineer in the United States, which highly interested my father. Working or living in the United States carried the sort of prestige my father was looking for. What I wanted in the man who would be my potential life partner, was of no concern to my father. They had decided on my marriage before I had even seen or met the man, without a word from me regarding what I wanted. I knew nothing about the man and had not even seen a picture of him. When my father told me, I had no choice, to back off and that he had made the decision for me; I was in shock. In that moment of fear, shock, and anger, I found strength and clarity of thought. Though an endless stream of tears rolled down my cheeks and fear and anger filled my system, my thoughts were crystal clear. *The best thing I could do is to get to know the guy and think and decide wisely. My father will arrange a marriage that make him look the most prestigious in others' eyes. He will not check anything more about the guy out of not caring about my life. If I blindly rejected this arrangement, somehow getting out of it, my father will simply do it all over again, and next time this could get worse*, I thought.

The man my father had arranged for me to marry came over, with his family, to meet me, and we had a long conversation. From the little I got to know of him in that conversation, he seemed like a good guy. I told him I wanted to complete my education before getting married and asked him if I could have some time to decide regarding our marriage, and he agreed. As he left, my father went after him and told him he would make sure I agreed to the marriage, telling his family to proceed with the preparations. I had not said yes to the marriage yet, and this worried my father.

The would-be groom was surprised to hear my father's comments. In our community, girls were always given the freedom of choice regarding marriage. Parents usually arranged the meeting between the two people, but the decision whether to marry or not, was made by the man and woman after they meet and talk. The meeting is arranged, but not the marriage—especially in the matriarchal Nair society to which we belong, forced marriages are unheard of. My father's actions made my would-be husband realize that something was wrong. When we met again, he told me not to give in to the pressure I was experiencing from my father. He insisted that we proceed only with my full consent. I was glad to see the good nature of this man and fell in love with him. I agreed to the marriage. I felt extremely lucky that this man showed up that day – a good man. If not, what would have happened? I do not dare to think, it scares me.

Every being in nature has a right to choose its life partner. How can my father take this right away from me, without caring about my life? America was my father's dream. It would bring him reputation, and he had much more in mind. His strategies for what he wanted included everything except me and my happiness. He never cared about what I wanted or how he made me feel. I never crossed his mind once, and the way he treated me proved his lack of love for me. What was even worse, was his complete denial that he had forced me once I agreed to the marriage. I had enough, and I could take no more. I felt lucky that the man who he had arranged was a good guy, though my father never cared to check anything about him. My life would have been very different if someone else had shown up that day, since my father cared the least about me and my life.

Some communities around the world will approve of actions such as those of my father. People will listen to such stories and say, *"Girls aren't smart enough to get things right, so parents decide for them. So what?"* Most of these people believe marriage is the offloading of a father's responsibility, handing her off to a man who can take care of her from that point forward. They do not believe girls, like boys, are fully capable of taking care of themselves and they do not believe in giving girls freedom of choice. Many girls go through forced marriages in many communities all around the world. It is shocking to see parents give in to such beliefs, without caring about their own children.

My arranged marriage changed the way I felt about my parents. Every cell in my body felt the anger and betrayal that I felt. My parents treated me like a second-class human being all because I am a girl. When dealing with people we love, we exercise care for them. When we ignore their feelings, emotions, and hopes for their future—when we use them to please us, is it love? Such actions do not come from a place of love. It comes from a place of ego. My anger was a thorn within me, spreading like an infection. It was eating me from within, and I soon realized that I was hurting myself by creating memories of these incidents. These memories would not leave me, it would chase me all the time, like a tiger hunting down its prey. I could not stop replaying the tape of these painful memories in my mind, putting myself in a bad emotional state.

I got married after I completed my education, and came to United States with my husband, where I started a new life. I wanted to forget what had happened and move on with my life. But that was not always possible. I wanted to believe that my parents had made an honest mistake and that they loved me. However, many incidents followed, which hurt me further. To top it off one person who came in as a new addition to extended family caused a lot more issues in my life. This person wanted money, power, and control. Often people who are looking for power and control use abuse as a tool. Abuse gives ego a feeling of superiority, and it makes the person feels powerful while hurting others. This person in my extended family chose this path and I was on the receiving end. This person felt the need to make me powerless and voiceless to achieve financial motives. "I will abuse you like this all your life, and you will neither have any power nor voice in your life.", this person told me once directly. Luckily, I was not around this person for too long, as this person was not part of my immediate family. However, even from a distance this person would influence people close to me, by creating misunderstanding, giving wrong information and advices, with an intention of creating problems in my life. People who are extremely manipulative often have great convincing skills, and it was shocking to see how false narratives were made to look perfectly valid and convincing. At some point, I could not take it anymore, and I was spiraling down emotionally. No one around me understood the gravity of the situation since this person handled it well in front of others.

The personality this person displayed in front of the world was such a caring one – it was a great drama that was made to look real. I only had the universal energy to turn to, for help. As always when I really needed help, doors open for me, and so it did again this time. Once again, I experienced the power of divine grace.

It took me a long time to realize that I am, and always have been, enough. To expect love from those who do not want to love me is foolish. Expecting them to change and bending backwards to show them how good I am, hoping they will stop the wrong behavior, and love me, was only causing me more pain. Family and extended family should stand by us in times of need and bring a smile on our faces. But when people in the family rob us of our smile, why should we remain close with them? My belief in some family and extended family members started to fade away. I realized that some people are the way they are, and they would never see or accept me for who I am. We are different, and I cannot let their ways ruin my life. They are living in a world of their beliefs, and they do not want to come out of it. Few others in my family and extended family, have been there for me all my life, supporting me mentally and emotionally through the challenging times. They have taught me through their actions, that my family should consist of people who love me, regardless of who they are. I realized those who were only hurting me, one way or another, need to be kept at a distance for me to move on with my life.

I practiced chanting and meditation which gradually helped me to stop feeling miserable and angry. I realized that no one had the right to hurt me, irrespective of who they are. We are divine beings and we need to love and respect each other, and the divine in us will not let us hurt each other. When people are hurting others that just means their actions are not guided by the divine. I also realized that

I do not need love and acceptance from others if I am able to love and accept myself. People have every right to choose, and if some people choose not to love me, I need to respect their decision and move on. I should not stick around them and demand their love. Instead, I should know I am enough and love myself. I understood for the first time, we should admire our own good nature instead of relying on others. We should stop expecting love from others and know how wonderful we are and try to be our own best friend.

Why did it take me so long to understand this? I was taught that loving myself was selfish, and that if others could not love me, that meant I was bad. When we are programmed to think this way, we live our lives trying to please others around us. We cannot live with the feeling that we are bad – it makes us miserable. However, If people can convince us that we are bad, because we didn't listen to them, we would spent the rest of our life trying to please them, doing exactly what they want, as a way to feel better about ourselves. What a powerful way of controlling others. The seed of control is planted in the mind of every child with simple, accusatory statements, and the child comes under control with ease. We are only labelled "good" if we please others. If we please ourselves and listen to our inner guidance, we are labelled selfish and "bad." I discovered this profound insight when I began to see my familial relationships in a new light. I stopped trying to please people and started focusing on my responsibilities and the things that give me peace and joy. I ignored the noise people were making in the background to try and disturb my mental state to get me under control. I kept my peace as much as possible, even when I was surrounded by people, who tried to disturb me mentally and take my power away. I learned to simply ignore and walk away without letting any of their words bother me beyond a point.

I also learned the true meaning of the word forgiveness. Forgiveness does not mean forgetting what happened and returning to the people who have hurt us. Forgiveness, in its true sense, is meant to heal us by releasing the pain from our systems. Forgiveness is an antidote to grief and pain, and that is it. It does not mean we have to make peace with the other person after what we have been through. Forgiveness means not letting anything or anyone negatively impact us. It means clearing our systems of pain, not letting the poison stay inside and ruin us. It means keeping our happiness in our control, not giving control to others. To do this, we must not let the actions of others hurt us. Those who hurt us want us to believe that we are bad, and they want to blame us for all the wrong things in life. But the choice is yours. Are you going to believe them? Forgiveness is not believing the false narratives.

The term "forgive and forget" does not mean what happened is alright. It means the only person we need to make peace with is ourselves, and we can achieve that by erasing the memory of the incident, after reflecting on what we learned from the incident. Every bad experience is a lesson, we just need to learn that lesson and move on. Every wound has a gift hidden inside it—a gift of awareness. We need to take the gift from the experience and throw away the rest. We are all wonderful people, and whatever incidents we had experienced weren't here to hurt us but to teach us. Seeing painful experiences through this lens removes the toxins from our systems, and that is the purpose of forgiveness.

I was recently listening to an interview of a girl who escaped the FLDS religious group. What the girls in this group experienced in the name of religious beliefs was too horrific for me to even listen to. In the name of God, girls were brutally gang raped and beaten daily. In the FLDS polygamy system, here in the United States, this behavior was normal. Kids born into this society thought that this is how life is supposed to be—this was how to treat women—because they had never seen or experienced anything different. The few who escaped saw a whole new world, with the help of volunteers who took care of these escaped children. How could these girls ever forgive the people in their lives after living a life of constant sexual and physical abuse, from the time of childhood? Such abuse creates intense pain, and if we do not learn to forgive our wrong doers, the pain can paralyze us for the rest of our lives.

We need to move forward knowing that there are people who lack understanding and empathy, because of which they choose to hurt others. We need to see the whole situation in such a way that we gain clarity into who the other person really is, allowing us to realize that whatever happened is not our fault. The biggest responsibility we have in life is to love ourselves and those who loves us, regardless of who they are. Our culture and religion may or may not guide us right, but we have a responsibility to choose the good aspects of culture and religion and leave out the rest. Religious and cultural teachings have been mistranslated and misinterpreted numerous times. If we cannot identify cultural and religious rights and wrongs, it will guide us in the wrong direction, and we will get hurt. In the case of the FLDS religious group, women are taught to believe that they would please God only if they agreed to sexual abuse and violence at the hands of men in their family and in their community. The FLDS silenced, and continues to silence, girls by saying that speaking up is a sin, no matter how much violence and abuse is suffered.

Forgiveness does not come easy when you go through such abuse. But we need to keep practicing forgiveness to move forward in our lives. We need to lift the weight off our hearts, opening them up, to make our lives better through forgiveness. Forgiveness is a process in which we accept that whatever happened was wrong and whoever hurt us was on the wrong side of things. It is understanding that we cannot let someone else's actions toward us bring us down in life. It is understanding that we need to convert the painful energy within us into strength that can take us to a happy and successful life. Forgiveness is a way of transforming pain into strength and learning from it. It is a way of taking care of ourselves and finding happiness by letting the pain flow out of us, filling our lives with hope and dreams instead. Forgiveness is using the painful energy as the strength required to work harder than ever, experiencing the wonders that life offers us by focusing on the present and being hopeful for the future.

When I look back at my life, painful experiences have helped me to be the person I am today. They helped me understand life better, and I am a far better person because I had those experiences. Would I trade my life experience for a chance at a more loving life experience? Looking back, I think that would be a bad idea, because I would not be this person without that experience. What is more important than the pain, is what I learned from it. The lessons I learned are far more valuable than the pain I went through. Though it was not easy to overcome some of the experiences, I look back and see the profound lessons life has taught me, and I could have never learned these lessons otherwise. Pain forces us to think differently and see things in a way we have never seen before. That is the reason life throws challenges at us, forcing us to expand our minds, leave our old ways behind, and become better human beings. Pain comes with the reward of awareness.

Today, I see the gift of my wounds. I am grateful that I was born in the time and place I was, and I am grateful to have experienced so many wonderful things in my childhood. I am grateful I had just enough negative experiences to help me get to where I am today. I am grateful I did not suffer like many children who have gone through extreme abuse and trauma. I am grateful I experienced a childhood. I am grateful that my parents took care of me and educated me, despite seeing me as less worthy. I believe that whatever happened in my life happened for a good reason. My father and few others in my family behaved the way they did because they did not know any better. They were blinded by their beliefs, and they followed it like many others did, thinking it is the right way. I share my experience and views so that people may understand why it is important to think for themselves instead of following established beliefs. If any father who believes his daughter is less capable of achieving success, can read these pages and understand that his beliefs will not serve him or his daughter, this book has served its purpose.

Looking back at my life, I see the divine force at play. This life has been quite a journey, and I am grateful for all the experience along the way. The gratitude I feel for all that life has given me, has washed away the pain and anger from my system. I have learned to be grateful and view my painful experiences through a positive lens to see the true purpose of those experiences. I am also aware that my experiences are not so bad, when compared to what so many innocent children are experiencing around the world. At this point in life, my heart is full of peace and gratitude, and I am enjoying the ride. The practice of peace and gratitude has taken me to a place of bliss. I have started to experience a state of profound joy, and when I am in this state of joy, the world around me looks brighter and beautiful. It is as if the colors of the trees and everything in nature are enhanced, as if it is touched by a divine light. Maybe this joy and feeling of bliss and beauty are what many describe as heaven on earth? Forgiveness and gratitude have taken me to this place of bliss, and I want to continue practicing gratitude to remain in this wonderful state of bliss.

CHAPTER 9

THE DIVINE GIFT OF LIFE

Looking back at my life, I wonder what would have happened to me if I was like the girls around me growing up, who listened and obeyed their parents without thinking and reasoning for themselves. Most of us were taught that obeying and pleasing our families were the most important qualities in a girl, and most girls believed this, trading their lives and dreams to please their families, and others around them. Girls were made to believe that marriage could provide their dream life, which was part of the reason why some girls walked easily into it. No girl was taught the dangers of life, such as if you end up in the wrong relationship. They also were not equipped with an education, to support themselves in case things went wrong. All of them were given false notions of married life. Many girls were taught they would marry a prince charming who would make their life a heaven on Earth. Girls who believed this narrative and dreamed of a wonderful family life, often learned the reality of life too late. Many girls whose marriages ended in divorce struggled to care for their kids financially. Girls from rich families have ended up in extreme poverty after some crises in life like death or divorce. They were left with no money or education and struggled to support their kids after such an unexpected turn in their lives. It was too painful to watch. Many such incidents surrounded me, but surprisingly, no one seemed to notice, or no one cared. If these girls entered marriage after receiving a proper education, they could have supported themselves and their kids financially, but their parents failed to think.

It was shocking to see how some societies were ignoring many issues caused by this outdated practice and beliefs. Though these incidents shocked me constantly, nothing shocked me more than an incident I witnessed when I was around ten years of age.

I was home alone one day, when the doorbell rang. I peeked through the window and saw a young mother with a three-to-four-month-old baby in her arms. Soon, four other kids—boys and girls, ages two through eight—came up and stood by my window, helplessly looking at me. The mother told me her husband—the father of these children—had abandoned them, and they had no money and nowhere to go. My ten-year-old self was in shock hearing the news and seeing these kids. *How could anyone do this to their own children?* I could not understand.

A month later, I saw the woman and her children again. This time, they were in the same clothes and a very bad state, begging on the street. Seeing them in that state, shook me to my core. I always knew that marriage was all my parents had in mind for me, but seeing that woman and her five kids, I promised myself that I would never let myself or my children be financially helpless. It was a wake-up call to take care of myself. The woman reflected a possible future for any girl who entered a marriage without an education and financial independence. I knew that my parents, like many others, would only care about improving their reputation through my marriage. How my life would turn out after the marriage was not a thought that entered their minds. *If they find me a bad husband, I might end up like that woman*, I thought. I realized that education and financial independence were vital for any girl to avoid such dangers. This realization created a fear in me that I couldn't let go of, until I completed my education.

The image of the abandoned women and her five kids, begging in the street, remains in my memory forever. Realizing that the story society tells girls about marriage is far from the truth, gave me the courage to fight all the obstacles that stood in my path. My path wasn't clear; many thorns along the way hurt me and challenged me, leaving me with wounds. I was constantly told I was not good enough. But no matter how much I was put down, I never once doubted myself. I told myself, *I can do it. All I need to do is figure out how.*

My parents were often taken aback by my courage and determination. They knew I would hold on to what I wanted in life, no matter how much they pushed against it. I made it in life because I was determined to make it; I couldn't imagine my life otherwise. My courage was my life's best companion. If I would have given up my fight at some point, I would be living like a zombie, with dreams shattered, believing I am not good enough. Believing girls and women are weak, living a life overrun by shame and depression. This is how many extremely skilled and talented women are living today. I know many of these women closely, and they are part of the reason why I fought so hard for myself. Society forced them into lives they never wanted to live by making them believe they were not good enough.

How can anyone who believes they are not good enough be happy? No wonder this world is starving for happiness. If a wife or a mother is unhappy, she cannot bring happiness into her home. I heard someone say, *"Women are the light of the house."* I wish the world understood the profound meaning of this statement. However, many of the world's societies keep their women and girls in darkness, turning off the light of the family. In modern days, women can, and actively do put food on the table, care for their kids, complete the household chores, and much more, and still the world fails to see the scope of her role. Instead, women are constantly looked down on, in many societies, as someone who is weak and less worthy.

In nature, only humans feel this way about the female gender. How does mother nature see the females? She trusts females' abilities and has entrusted the females with the most important role—procreation. Producing children and sustaining the cycle of life is mother nature's most important task. She cannot risk her process of creation by giving it to anyone other than those strong enough to accomplish the task. Who did mother nature assign this task to? Who does the force of nature trust with procreation, caring for the young, and sustaining life? The males are given the role of protecting the family, because the young ones and mother need protection and help. When nursing, females need a helping hand in raising their young, providing for the family and protecting them from any external danger. Males take up this role. Nature gives males physical strength for the purpose of protecting, and nature gave females mental strength and the ability to love and care for the young. Both males and females have their roles in nature, and neither role is better than the other.

When people and societies choose to think out of the purely egocentric desire to be superior, the world around them does not progress. The main point of all religions, which is so often missed today, is to show love and compassion, but all anyone seems to be interested in is laying down rules. Most people blindly believe what their religion teaches and never once validate what they hear. A wise human is always curious to learn, think, and reason before believing. Harmful social, religious, and cultural beliefs will not creep into our lives if we are wise to think and reason before believing and following.

Denying women their freedom and opportunity is the denial of basic human rights. Parents deny intelligent and talented girls their freedom of choice and education, because they see her as marriage material. This is not an act of love; it is a lack of love. The lack of love comes from a lack of understanding, but that does not justify such behavior. No one has the right to take away another's freedom simply because it is their child. Where there is love, such acts are not possible. Where such acts exist, there is no love, only ego exist. Love is caring for the other person, being a support to them, and helping them to live life with joy. When parents do things that take away their child's joy, how can it be love? A father free of ego cannot treat his daughter as a lesser being and deny her freedom. A father with the ability to think clearly will have the clarity and vision to see that such acts do not serve his daughter.

We need light to see in the world. In darkness, we do not know what exists around us. Similarly, when the human mind has a clear conscience, the awareness within will start to shine like a bright light. Awareness lets us see things clearly in life. Awareness acts as a light for our thoughts, words, and action. The more we choose the right path, the brighter and brighter our awareness shines, helping us to distinguish between truth and lies, and helping us to see people for who they truly are. Taking the right path in life becomes easier when such clarity exists. True awareness dissolves ego, superiority, and all negative thoughts. It takes us to a place of inner contentment, peace, and well-being. We start to become calmer, smile more, and experience a profound sense of self-love. Most spiritual teachers have said that heaven and the kingdom of God is within each of us. These words make sense when we can experience the profound feeling of consistent peace and joy within. However, people who live lives filled with ego and negativity cannot experience inner peace and joy, which is why they do not believe it. They choose to stick with their false beliefs and live as victims of their egocentric minds. They will not have inner peace and will continue to live a life of fear so long as they are motivated by ego.

On the other hand, people who live their lives in awareness never have such fear. They experience inner peace and do not fear how they are perceived by the world around them. Their emotions are always balanced. They never bow in front of anyone out of fear or shame, and they do not soar high out of pride. People living in awareness perceive life as it is, seeing creation's bigger picture in everyday life. They understand that our existence in the universe is like a pebble of sand on the ocean floor. They know how fragile life is and that life energy is divine. They have love and respect for everything and everyone.

Each of our lives is our gift, and how we live it should be our choice. We must listen to what people say, but we should decide for ourselves if it makes sense to us before we choose to follow anything in life. Our lives are our own, and we cannot let others rob us of our lives in the name of family, religion, or culture. The divine gift of life is priceless, and it is gifted to us. It is ours to value, cherish, and love. We must use it to experience joy and bring joy to others. We should not use it to feed the ego—ours or others. We need to own our lives and take full responsibility for them. It is our responsibility to take care of our lives. If we throw away our lives to please others, by living the lives others want us to live, ignoring what we want, we are throwing away the most precious gift the universal forces have given us. We would be wasting a divine opportunity. We must choose to treat our lives as a gift and value it more than anything else. We must love ourselves. We are here, with this opportunity in life, because a force of divine love gave it to us to experience, explore, and create. We are spiritual beings in human form, having a human experience. While still here, let us take the driver's seat and enjoy the ride. It might get rough at times and scare us at times, but it is just a ride. We will not get an opportunity to go back and do it all over again, at least not as the person we are now, so we must cherish every moment and gift ourselves with the best opportunities in this life, even if it means fighting some tough battles. It is all worth the ride.

CHAPTER 10

GET TO KNOW YOURSELF

I often wonder, *how did all this happen?* Everything looks like a miracle, to me. I completed my education, got a job I love, and I am living a happy life. Some call it luck, but I choose to call it grace—combined with the right attitude. Courage and persistence were key factors in my process of getting to where I am now, but I would not have made it without grace. Grace, combined with determination, brought me to my destination. I refused to give up whenever I failed, continuing to try again, till I succeeded.

Some girls I knew had to walk away from their dreams before they even got started. Unfortunately, they were "good girls" who listened and gave up their dreams to please others. I wish they knew what it feels like to achieve their dreams, but they never fought for themselves. I was not a so-called "good girl" because I fought for my dreams. I was called selfish for not obeying others and giving up my dreams. But unlike other girls, who believed these false narratives, these remarks made me think, *isn't it a selfish request to ask me to give up my dreams?* I felt it was. It was not selfish of me to have a dream for myself; what was selfish was asking me to give up my dreams. The true meaning of the term "selfish" does not apply to me. I know who I am, and if people label me as "selfish", as a way of trying to get me to do what they want, I will take that label and walk with it toward my dreams.

In many communities around the world, men feel the need to discriminate against women and put them down to feel powerful.

This belief exists in communities and families where men are told that listening to women makes them look like less of a man. These environments become a breeding ground for ego, forcing men to "be a man" in the wrong way. Around the world, women are abused because men believe a lack of love and compassion makes them look more like a man. Little do they realize that it is their ego causing them to buy into such wrong beliefs and external influences.

Truly strong men do not feel the need to boost their egos. They are aware of their strength and do not feel the need to prove they are strong. Trying to prove strength is a sign of weakness. It is fear and lack of belief in one's own strength that causes a man to act this way to "be a man". Strong men choose love and compassion, over ego and control. Strong men do not keep ego as their companion, only weak ones do. Only strong men can stand hand in hand with women and help women achieve their dreams. A weak man can never stand by a woman, because he lacks the strength and courage to do so. For a man to stand by a wife and daughter—to support her as a husband or as a father—takes courage. Fathers who see their daughters as equals, giving their daughters freedom and opportunity, are heroes. They are men with courage, and their courage is the only reason these men do not fear standing by the women in their lives. Love makes life beautiful, not ego and control. We must teach love and practice it without fear, dropping our egos.

I feel so grateful for my life. I am thankful for the divine grace— the life energy—that guided me. I have experienced it at every turning point in my life. But while growing up, for a long time, I did not believe in anything more than what I could perceive with my physical senses. Science was my ultimate truth for the first few years of my life. As a child, I saw my great grandmother perform her daily prayers, and I used to sit with her while she chanted and meditated. I just wanted to be in her presence. I would imitate her like a monkey, not knowing anything about what she was asking me to do. She never forced her beliefs on me, she just told me stories that instilled good values in me.

When I was around twelve years old, my great grandmother was diagnosed with chickenpox. Though she recovered from the disease, she was weak and bedridden. One morning, to everyone's surprise, she woke up and said she was perfectly fine. She asked my aunt to get her warm water for a bath. She bathed, smeared her forehead with sandalwood paste and collected the water and holy basil leaves she needed to perform her prayers. As she was chanting her mantras, looking at the rising sun, she began to lean over to one side. Her son, who was sitting next to her, saw this and moved from his chair, fearing that she might fall. He stretched his hands, and as he did, she fell into his arms and took her last breath, her gaze still set upon the rising sun. Her death was unexpected, and I lost my most favorite person in the world that day.

My great-grandmother's death caused me to reexamine my belief to only trust the five senses of the physical body. I began looking for answers in Hindu texts. I read books by spiritual teachers and saints, which introduced me to the concept of a person's conscience. The first teacher I read was Swami Vivekananda. His writings and teachings were simple and clear for me to understand at that young age. Later, I was introduced to materials from all over the world. I enjoyed those materials, and they often answered my many questions. I found one common message in all the teachings I read. Each text preached a message of love, compassion, gratitude, and a feeling of oneness. Yet despite this one message, which resonates in all spiritual teachings, religious groups around the world are practicing something that goes against this message.

Most people cannot see the pain and suffering of their fellow human beings, and they cannot understand the meaning of compassion and gratitude. We live our lives in such arrogance, with the egocentric belief of being all-powerful. We are obsessed with our bodies and physical appearance, and we associate ourselves with these bodies and material things more than anything else. We believe only that which we can perceive using our five senses. But what if there is more? What if the universe is more energy than matter? What if matter is only a temporary state of energy? What if the universe is filled with intelligent energy? The truth is, we do not know the answer to these questions. Why would anything intelligent reveal itself to such arrogant beings like humans, who watch murder for entertainment, and kill in the name of peace? However, religions are based in the belief that we have it all figured out.

The practice of believing without thinking is hurting humanity, yet we are taught not to question our beliefs. Others do not want us questioning their teachings because they want to use us to achieve their desires in life. If we think before we believe, their plans are at risk.

We should not follow anything on Earth without thinking first. We all come to the planet as equals, just at different times. The creator gives us the ability to think, question, and reason everything. But once we make it to Earth, we are taught not to use the precious gift of thought. What are people afraid of? If we think, question, and reason, we will see truth and light. The people who want to put us in darkness will always try to stop us from thinking. The choice is ours. Do we want to live happy, free lives? Or do we want to live lives of pleasing others, following their beliefs and practices? Each of us has the right to choose. Breaking the rules might be difficult, but wrong beliefs will also make for a more difficult life. Choosing old ways might look easy, but it is like entering a jungle because we believed someone, who told us the jungle is safe and free of danger. Once in the jungle, when we encounter danger, we are on our own to face it.

Every major decision we make will have a profound impact on our lives. Decisions guide our lives toward or away from who we want to be or do in life. They take us toward or away from happiness and well-being.

Choose what is right and live life with good intention. We must choose right thoughts, words, and actions to achieve happiness. But we choose to worry, complain, and focus on things that make us unhappy. We are addicted to our unhappy way of life. We must work towards changing our thoughts words and action to a more positive one. Ask ourselves how much time we have in this life. If today is our last day, how will we value our time here on Earth? The truth is, today could be the last day for any of us. But we deny this truth, the reason we often focus on the negative aspect of life. At any point in life what makes us miserable is not what is external but what is churning up internal, in your thoughts. In any circumstance you can keep your calm and not let things bother you if you think right and focus positively. How many of us can do that? Happiness is a choice - to choose right and focus right. It is an attitude of picking the good from the bad and focusing on good.

Most people believe that life is the beginning and the end. But does death really mean our end? Is there anything more to us than our physical bodies? Let us examine. When we listen to a piece of information, we all hear that piece of information the same way; however, we process information much differently from each other. Why? Because the intelligence within each of us helps us process the information. Each of our intelligence is unique, so the way we each think, and process information is unique. If there is such an intelligence, which is eternal, then why don't we remember our past lives?

Each one of us go to sleep every night and wake up the next day with the same worries we had the day before. We have bills to pay, work to complete, exams to pass, and much more. Now, imagine if we were to wake up and all the problems from the previous day had vanished. No one would remember what had happened the day before, and we would each get a fresh start. How would people choose to live that day? Better or worse? A worry free life will be definitely better.

We all start with a clean slate in this life. It is so much better. It is a fresh start, for a new journey. We are born with a body, and we are ready to begin our life experience. Planet Earth consist of people who are evolved in their thoughts and people who are at very low levels of thought evolution. It is a tough place to be, but a great place to learn and grow. The diversity of intelligence on Earth is the reason we sometimes struggle to make certain people understand certain things. People understand based on the evolutionary level of their intelligence. People at higher levels of intelligence understand things far better than people at lower levels of intelligence. To reach higher levels, we must learn through life experiences. Words cannot teach, but life experiences can. Sometimes we see people who lack love and empathy for others. How will they change? Can we transform people by words? Not really. The only way they will change is when they feel the pain of another through life experience. The feelings and emotions create a certain memory of the experience, which stays with us. Even if we forget about the experience, we know how it feels to be there. The memory of that feeling makes us a better person. We now have compassion and empathy for the other, since we now know the pain of others.

The wide variety of intelligence on Earth also create the lack of understanding we often experience. People find it hard to understand one another, because they have different levels of intelligence and understanding. What makes sense to some people does not to another. This is due to the diversity of intelligence. The intelligence that people are born with is unique to each of us, and age and education have nothing to do with it. A child may have immense intelligence and be able to see life with a clarity that most adults around them may not even be close to understanding. Most of what this child has to say, may not be understood by adults around due to the intelligence gap. When what the child is saying cannot be perceived by the adults, in most cases the adults will choose to see the child as weird rather than intelligent. So, the belief that we are better, or more intelligent, because we are older does not make sense when we consider the evolution of the human conscience and intelligence.

We are all in pursuit of happiness and happiness is vital to our systems—mind and body. Being happy is what allows us to fulfill our true potential. Our lives' purpose can be achieved through the path of happiness. Positive emotions, such as joy, enthusiasm, and contentment, are flashlights that guide us to our lives' purpose. Our dreams, however big or small, are our path to happiness. If we deviate from our purpose, we are unhappy. It is up to us, to choose well-being, by thinking happy thoughts, or to choose sickness, by focusing on negatives. A happy mind brings us joy and clarity, which is a wonderful state to be in. It is the experience of heaven on earth – a state of bliss. But the path to heaven on earth is not easy. Beliefs, rules, relationships, culture, and much more create many obstacles. Our happiness depends on what we choose from the buffet life throws at us. It requires no effort to pick wrong things from this buffet; those come easy. But if we insist on picking only the good, it is tough but worth it. If we make the right choice, we will have the taste of bliss. It is up to us to choose.

We must take ownership of our lives and not let someone else decide for us. Just like we each have different taste buds, each of us has different likes, dislikes, and dreams. Only we know the taste we love. If we let someone else pick for us, we may not like the taste it creates in our lives. So, we must choose for ourselves and make the right decisions for our lives, to be happy.

Know that women—or anyone deemed as "different"—are not lesser in any way. People who tell us we are not capable do not know us well enough. They may be trying to take control of our lives because they do not see us for who we really are. It is up to us to live our lives to our true potential. We cannot wait for permission to take charge of our lives. If we wait, we will never get it. The truth is, most people like controlling others, and they fear giving us control of our own lives. They are afraid of our inner strength and will keep saying we are weak and not good enough. They will laugh at our opinions and never accept us for who we are. The question is, are we going to trust them or trust ourselves? Life is about taking a leap of faith. We must believe in ourselves and take the leap. We cannot change others, but we can change ourselves by choosing what is right for us. By changing our lives, we can change the world around us. Let us step up our game and take charge. This life is all ours, so let us enjoy this ride of life.

CHAPTER 2

1. DR. Joe Dispenza, Becoming Supernatural: how common people are doing the uncommon (Carlsbad, California: Hay House 2017). Chapter 2: The present moment: Page 46.

2. DR. Joe Dispenza, Becoming Supernatural: how common people are doing the uncommon (Carlsbad, California: Hay House 2017). Chapter 2: The present moment: Page 47.

CHAPTER 6

1. Super Soul Sunday on OWN network aired on Oct 11, 2015. http://www.oprah.com/own-super-soul-sunday/ oprah-and-nobel-peace-prize-winner-malala-yousafzai-video

2. Stanford commencement speech on June 12, 2005, at Stanford University CA. https://www.ted.com/talks/ steve_jobs_how_to_live_before_you_die

CPSIA information can be obtained
at www.ICGtesting.com
Printed in the USA
LVHW020738101120
671146LV00007B/466